REMEMBERING ERNIE KUCK

REMEMBERING ERNIE KUCK

Cattleman, Historian, Philanthropist

Marilyn G. Ericksen with Irene Hill

mill city press • minneapolis, mn

Copyright © 2015 by Marilyn G. Ericksen

Mill City Press, Inc.
322 First Avenue N, 5th floor
Minneapolis, MN 55401
612.455.2293
www.millcitypublishing.com

All rights reserved. No part of this publication may be reproduced, stored in a retrieval system, or transmitted, in any form or by any means, electronic, mechanical, photocopying, recording, or otherwise, without the prior written permission of the author.

Cover Image - *Ernie Kuck Memorial* (1997) at the Wasco County Historical Museum/Columbia Gorge Discovery Center, The Dalles, Oregon, created by artist Jeff Stewart. Photo by Jonathan Hill.

ISBN-13: 978-1-63413-512-2
LCCN: 2015906549

Cover Design by Colleen Rollins
Typeset by B. Cook

Printed in the United States of America

*It takes courage to grow up
and become who you really are.*

—E. E. Cummings

CONTENTS

Foreword		ix
Preface		xi
Acknowledgments		xv
Introduction: The Dalles		3
1	Ernie's Beginnings	9
2	Screaming Meemies and a Grub Hoe	15
3	Ernie's First Love	23
4	Jimmy	27
5	Another Ernie	35
6	Kuck & Bonney Sporting Goods	39
7	Mutual Respect	47
8	"But I Pay More Taxes!"	51
9	The "Double Lazy A" Cattle Company	61
10	Springs and Ponds	69
11	The Great Cattle Drive	75
12	"I Don't Think It's Near That Funny!"	83
13	Accidental Money	87
14	"Now Don't Tell"	93
15	Another New Friend	99
16	Ernie's Second Love	103
17	Five-Star Photographer	110
18	Ernie and Friends	117

19	"That's My Ernie!"	120
20	"Save Your Money"	124
21	A Lifelong Collector	129
22	"Too Many Years Have Passed"	133

Appendix A: E. A. Kuck Land Purchases — 139
Appendix B: Water Sources — 147

FOREWORD

This book is about a man of small stature and strong ethical principles. He chose to be known as a common man; he never actively sought attention. Comfortable with silence, he could ride horseback with someone all day and never say more than half a dozen words. He was a keen observer of wildlife, livestock, and people. He understood these beloved fellow creatures with a strength of perception that was unusually accurate.

Everyone knew that Ernest Kuck (rhymes with *luck*) was a well-to-do cattleman, but no one knew just *how* well-to-do until he passed away and left nine million dollars designated to construct and maintain a Wasco County Museum.

Everyone knew Ernest Kuck as Ernie. This remarkable man often said, "I made more money accidentally than I ever did on purpose." Therein lies the content of *Remembering Ernie Kuck: Cattleman, Historian, Philanthropist.*

—Wendy Best

PREFACE

In the 1980s, while I was recording the stories of seniors in Wasco County, June Martin (a lifelong resident of The Dalles) suggested to me that Ernie Kuck knew lots of local history and had plenty of stories to tell. I approached him and learned that he was willing to visit but that he didn't want to be taped. "It would sound like I, I, I, and I don't want that!" he said firmly. I made notes to the best of my ability.

When Ernie died, his unexpected bequest for a Wasco County Historical Museum surprised a lot of people because he had been known to many as a "loner." Overnight, this "tightwad" suddenly became a magnanimous philanthropist. Although his contributions to struggling farmers or organizations that needed a bailout had been happening for a long time, he always accompanied his loans or gifts with the admonition, "Don't tell anybody."

My interest in Ernie had been awakened by my conversations with him in the early 1990s. I really knew very little about him even though he was married to Helen, my mother's sister. Helen and Ernie were married in 1922, one month before I was born. Helen's mother had decided that her youngest, the light of her life, should marry a professional man, and Ernie did not meet her criteria. She opposed the union, but had to live with it.

My father and brother were drowned in a fishing accident on the Deschutes River when I was seven. Mother returned to her earlier profession of teaching. Ernie was focused on his ranches and his cattle, so he had little in common with a widowed primary school teacher. Helen and her mother (my grandmother) were frequent visitors to our home, but Ernie and his son, James Henry, called "Jimmy," were usually "at the ranch." Thus my knowledge of this uncle was largely secondhand.

When the Columbia Gorge Discovery Center opened, with the Wasco County Historical Museum (that Ernie had made possible) housed in the same building, I elected to gather as much information about Ernie Kuck as I could. I interviewed over forty people: those for whom he had worked in his youth; those who had worked for him or with him; friends from the Elks Club; and the Fort Dalles Riders. Each person had a little different opinion of Ernie—each saw a different facet of his personality. He became a challenging enigma for me, and I wanted to know him better.

This search for the real Ernie Kuck has been a lengthy one, interrupted by the loss of my husband, Walter; by several surgeries; and by my move to Down Manor, a retirement facility in Hood River. While at Down Manor, I became an enthusiastic member of a writing group. Soon I found myself delving into my file of transcribed "Ernie notes." They were so interesting! I created little vignettes for the writing group. In my mind, these disconnected stories became a book.

Faced with a mounting numbers of essays—some repetitious, a few dull, and some that sparkled with Ernie's

Preface

personality—I was overwhelmed. My daughter, Irene Hill, came to my rescue. She helped me to evaluate my stories and to make them into a connected account. I am grateful and deeply indebted to her for the assistance she provided. Thank you, Irene. We did it!

—Marilyn Ericksen

ACKNOWLEDGMENTS

This book is a compilation of memories and stories gathered over the last two decades from many sources. People that I spoke to or corresponded with include: Terry Alfson, investment broker; Betty Broer, U.S. Bank employee; John Buckman, forester; Norma McDonald Clark, neighbor; Carol Daniels, friend and confidant; Patty Gray, Carrie Kuck's granddaughter; Wayne Huskey, acquaintance; Sandy Macnab, Wasco County extension agent; Clayton McCall, Wasco County road department supervisor; Chuck Petroff, cattleman; Max Post, son of Carrie Kuck; Norma Shull, wife of Vernon Shull, an Oregon State highway engineer; Dee Thompson, member of Good Sam Club; Monte Wasson, son of Mannie Wasson, who rode with Ernie; and Linda Miller Wilson, daughter of Joe and Pat Miller.

Much of this book is based on tape-recorded interviews of Ernie's friends and acquaintances that I conducted shortly after Ernie's death in 1992. Although many of these folks have since passed on, the recordings have been digitized and are now archived at the Columbia Gorge Discovery Center in The Dalles, Oregon. I interviewed: Garth Bonney, a saddle maker and son of Ralph, and his wife, Evalyn; Frank Falbo,

Elks member and confidant; Jake Grossmiller, friend who helped with cattle; Roger Howe, insurance agent; Vernie Jarl, padlock collector; Lucile Ketchum, widow of Bill Ketchum Jr.; Bill and Shelia Markman, friends who purchased Eight Mile Ranch; Joe Miller, son of Jesse Miller, and his wife, Pat, both cattlemen; the Nagle sisters, neighbors who helped with cattle: May Nagle Proctor, Helen Nagle Sallee, Florence Nagle Walls; Ernie Rhodes, Grange member who helped with cattle; Wilma Roberts, photography mentor; Bob Sallee, son of Helen Sallee, neighbor who helped with cattle; Gladys Seufert, photographer and local history buff; Floyd Tibbets, friend who leased Eight Mile Ranch; Paul Vogt, local doctor and history buff; Elden and Joan Wagenblast, friends who leased Deschutes Ranch; and Mannie and Zelta Wasson, friends who helped with cattle.

The development of all these stories into book form could never have happened without the help of many people. Having heard and written many of the stories about Ernie, it was invaluable to actually take tours of Ernie's Eight Mile Ranch with Bill Markman and Ernie's Chenowith holdings with John Fulton. John and Ruth (Tibbets) Fulton were also most generous in sharing pictures, Ernie's maps and a photocopy of his "Little Book," which repeatedly shed light on unanswered questions. Appreciation to David McGaughey at the Wasco County Clerk's Office for his patient assistance during a tedious search through Ernie's many title deeds, and to Laura Davies, HonPSA, Photographic Society of America historian, who did a manual search through old PSA journals that had not yet been digitized. Thanks to Rymmel Lovell for curating The Dalles School Districts' Archive Museum and thus preserving glimpses into Ernie's school days, and also to

Acknowledgments

Ben Beseda of Tenneson Engineering for helping with maps. Special gratitude to my wordsmith, Wendy Best, who initiated my writing experience at Down Manor, and then provided invaluable assistance in preparing the manuscript. Thanks to Paula Montgomery for doing a preliminary copy edit. I am indebted to the staff at Mill City Press for their patience, insights, and help in the publishing process.

This book could not have happened without the support of my children. Irene Hill faithfully listened to my short stories about Ernie and helped me formulate an outline for the book. She facilitated the computerized digital aspects of writing a book that are far beyond my ken. She researched answers to endless questions, created maps and gathered photos to illustrate life and times. Thanks to my daughter Evelyn Ana Moskowitz for her input and attention to detail (especially with the maps), and to my son, Dan Ericksen, for his support, encouragement and patience on this lengthy journey. The book has benefited from his thoughtful choice of words and his suggestions for revisions based on his familiarity with Wasco County, its people and its history.

Appreciation goes to Bill Dick and the Wasco County Historical Museum Board for their support and for permission to use photos of Ernie and information from his "Little Book." I also wish to acknowledge the Wasco County Historical Museum/Columbia Gorge Discovery Center, especially Carolyn Purcell and Katherine Purcell for their assistance in researching Ernie's life and collections and for permission to use four of the images for this book. And, finally, a special thanks to Jeffery Stewart for the cover image, featuring his deep-relief wall sculpture, *Ernie Kuck Memorial* (1997), displayed at the Wasco County Historical Museum. Jeff's artistic portrayal of Ernie herding cattle down Auction Yard Hill toward The Dalles conveys much about the character of the man.

REMEMBERING ERNIE KUCK

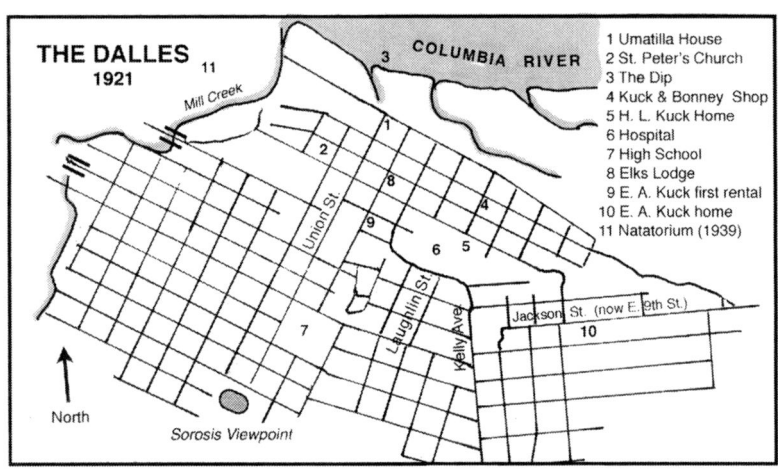

Map created by Irene Hill based on a map of The Dalles, 1921, by P. W. Marx, city engineer, archived at The Columbia Gorge Discovery Center, The Dalles, Oregon.

INTRODUCTION
The Dalles

Ernest Anderson Kuck's early life and development shaped his lifelong fascination with being out of doors, riding the hills where he could gaze at length on the unimpeded views of Mt. Hood and Mt. Adams. As a youngster, when he strongly felt the need to "get out of town" (one of his own favorite expressions), he contrived ways to spend time in the mountains, sometimes helping herd sheep, sometimes enjoying the solitude in one of the various line cabins. These were used by cattlemen whose herds grazed in the wild hills and valleys surrounding The Dalles, Oregon. To the west, forested mountains climbed up to the foothills of Mt. Hood. On the east, the rolling hills produced grain crops and served as winter pasture for Ernie's cattle.

During the early 1900s, the view from what is now Sorosis Memorial Viewpoint (the highest south elevation in The Dalles) included a panorama of the developing community along the big horseshoe bend of the Columbia River. Roads leaving town to the east and west led to outlying homesteads.

Looking from the viewpoint, one could see Union Street marking the east/west division of The Dalles. Other landmarks included a very large hotel—the "finest west of the Mississippi"—called the Umatilla House. Riverboats and the ferry tied up to a nearby dock so that passengers debarked close to the wraparound veranda on the establishment. The hotel boasted the most elegant board for room keys north of San Francisco and a handsome registration counter. The curving staircase in the lobby led to a sitting room for the ladies on the second floor. The men enjoyed a billiard room and a well-stocked bar watched over by a couple of discreetly carved nude figures on either side of the back wall. The huge dining room seated over 200 people.

Still, the hotel had a few drawbacks. When one registered, one rented a bed, not a room. Roommates were the luck of the draw. There were also an inordinate number of other residents: fleas, lice and bed bugs. The building survived several fires but was quickly rebuilt and sometimes enlarged. Wags in town lamented the hundreds of lives lost in the fires—referring to the insects. Before the Umatilla House was razed in 1929, folks gathered relics as souvenirs of the historic structure.

On Third Street, west of Union Street, an impressive spire topped with a six-foot rooster identified St. Peter's Catholic Church. On the north side of the street, a three-story brick building housed St. Mary's Catholic boarding school, which served the whole county.

Beyond the west edge of town lay a flat patchwork of "cheat grass" (a very hardy and wiry local type of wild grass) and basalt outcroppings interspersed with ponds and patches of sand. Two roads led west. On the south side of the flat, wheel tracks (later called Chenowith Road) followed the base of the hill. On the flat's north side, another set of tracks, avoiding the patches of basalt, loosely followed the course of the Columbia River and led to the fertile soil along the banks of Chenowith

Introduction

Creek. Continuing west, that road disappeared around Crates Point and later became known as Highway 30.

When he was a youth, Ernie and other vigorous young men held impromptu rodeos just south of the Sorosis viewpoint. They snubbed a "wild" horse up to one of their mounts, the riders formed a circle to create a boundary, and the broncbuster mounted. He either rode the horse or landed on the ground.

During the 1940s, the view from Sorosis revealed a city with a population of about 5,000 people. The city had grown slowly but steadily. The cheat grass disappeared as the civic clubs gradually raised money to develop Sorosis Park with lawn grass, a sprinkler system, and picnic tables. The newly completed Scenic Highway 30 (also known as "Lancaster's Road") made it possible for residents to drive to Portland. However, it took four hours on the narrow, curvy road with no shoulders. There was no other way for automobiles to traverse the Cascade Mountains between The Dalles and Portland.

The railroad entered town from the west on a long trestle that crossed the Mill Creek Delta, which fanned out as it approached the Columbia River. The south bank of the big river alternated between sandy beach and rigid basalt bluffs. Previous floods in The Dalles had forced businesses to move away from the waterfront and First Street. Most businesses were located on Second Street, also known as Scenic Highway 30.

The foot of Union Street had lost the Umatilla House, but the ferry dock remained. In the summer, kids swam in the Columbia at a nearby site known as the Dip, where there was a floating wooden platform with diving boards. In 1939, the city built a new, Olympic-sized swimming pool on West Second Street, making the Dip obsolete. A large dock on the riverfront accommodated oceangoing vessels that transported grain and other merchandise to Portland and beyond.

The Dalles gradually assumed a new identity as an agricultural and trade center. A somewhat motley assortment of immigrants and transients had either moved on or become responsible citizens.

Through the years, recurring floods had battered the city. In 1894, people used rowboats to navigate the city streets. Prior to a very bad flood in 1948, residents piled sandbags high to protect the town, but water broke through anyway and flooded the whole waterfront area. Floodwaters continued to roar on to Portland, Oregon, where they wiped out the whole community of Vanport.

After cleaning up in The Dalles, the city fathers bolstered the river's edge north of town by constructing permanent revetments using fill and riprap. To the west, they reshaped Mill Creek Delta to channel the creek's flow directly into the Columbia River. The train trestle was taken down. The filled areas became usable space, changing the appearance of the waterfront.

Bonneville Dam, constructed forty miles west of The Dalles and dedicated in 1937, proved so successful that the U.S. Army Corp of Engineers soon planned a similar project at The Dalles. The new dam would provide electrical power, prevent floods, be a source of water for irrigation, and enhance recreational opportunities.

The 1950s saw the start of two decades of construction. The Dalles Dam was built east of town. A toll bridge spanned the Columbia a short distance downstream from the dam, replacing the ferry that had tied up at the foot of Union Street for many years. Cheap electrical rates near the dam attracted power-hungry industries to consider locating at The Dalles.

Introduction

Harvey Aluminum, based in Torrance, California, constructed an aluminum reduction plant west of town between the Columbia River and Highway 30. It began operation in 1958. Within twenty years, the population doubled. Housing subdivisions appeared, one after another, in the hills east and southeast of town. Large homes quickly filled the lots by the Sorosis Park Viewpoint.

Little houses sprouted up along the Chenowith flat west of town—houses without city codes to guide the developing neighborhoods. The dirt streets had no sidewalks. The number of school-age children increased beyond the capacity of The Dalles School District #12 to absorb all the high school students. Since Harvey Aluminum's reduction plant paid significant property taxes into Chenowith School District #9, and a second high school was needed, the Chenowith school district built Wahtonka High School. The Dalles now had two high schools on Tenth Street, three miles apart.

Ernie Kuck witnessed all of these changes from his birth in 1896 to his death in 1992 at the age of 95. He lived and prospered in The Dalles and invested his life and fortune in the community.

The childhood home of Ernie Kuck at 4th
and Laughlin Streets in The Dalles, Oregon.

Photo from author's personal files

CHAPTER 1

Ernie's Beginnings

Ernest Anderson Kuck was born in The Dalles on July 29, 1896, to Henry Lincoln Kuck and his wife, Minnie Anderson Kuck. He was the couple's second son, born two years after Harry. The new baby was welcomed joyfully into the Kuck's lovely two-story home on East Fourth Street at Laughlin, two blocks south of his father's harness shop.

Ernie's early years centered around his home on Fourth Street. He explored the hillside behind his back yard where The Dalles General Hospital stood on top of an almost vertical wasteland. Little Ernie scrambled up the steep hill through cheat grass, dock, bindweed, and scrub oak that all vied for a secure footing. The area had been "salted" with some very interesting items from the hospital, such as prescription bottles with labels from various local drug stores. He examined the little bottles carefully before he carried them home to add to his collection. One unique, large bottle bore the label of Stubling Bottling Works, the former occupant of the building that Ernie's father, Henry Kuck, now occupied with his saddle and harness shop at Second and Laughlin Streets.

At that time, people often tossed unwanted items over a bank, down a hill, or into a creek. Without a garbage man with a scheduled route, getting rid of "junk" required a trip to the dump—a rat-infested, smelly pile of rotting waste. No one seemed to care that the hospital occasionally dumped refuse down the steep hillside, where it just disappeared among the weeds.

When Ernie was still quite young, adults began to appreciate him as a responsible helper. To help the saddle maker at his father's shop, he often kept an eye on the temperature of the solution used to soften the leather strips. On school days, Ernie came home for lunch—a walk of five or six blocks. After eating, he would often go lend a hand at the shop so a worker could eat lunch.

Ernie was a willing young fellow and eager to learn. He enjoyed making things, or helping others make things, that would last, developing standards of performance that served him well through the years. Although he learned how to do leather work, he had no interest in becoming a professional saddle maker or harness maker.

What Ernie loved was to "get out of town." At the age of eight, he owned a pony, which was boarded with all of the Kuck horses at a stable diagonally across the intersection from their home. It wasn't long before Ernie could saddle his mount and ride west about three miles to visit Uncle Fred and Aunt Nettie near the mouth of Chenowith Creek. Nettie Anderson Wetle was the sister of Ernie's mother. Ernie learned lots while helping on the Wetle farm. Uncle Fred raised an assortment of vegetables and sold them in town, but each variety from the truck garden required a custom-sized crate. Ernie learned how to build the wooden crates in assorted sizes, when to pick the produce, and how to pack it into the crates snugly, but not tightly enough to bruise the crisp, fresh vegetables.

Ernie's Beginnings

Uncle Fred maintained a herd of Black Angus cattle. Ernie learned how to care for stock, raise hay, and feed and pasture the animals. He especially liked working with the cattle. As he and Uncle Fred talked about stock, young Ernie's preference leaned toward the white-faced Hereford cattle.

George Anderson, also known as "Uncle Pete," was an excellent gunsmith. He constructed every part of his guns by hand, including the beautiful stocks, which were made of cherry wood from his own small orchard. While Uncle Pete made the gun barrels, Ernie provided the foot power on the pedal that ran the pulley that turned the lathe to ream out the interior of the barrel. Surely this sweat equity invested in perfectly made guns increased his appreciation of the end product.

Ernie treasured the guns that Uncle Pete left to him. In his later years, when he no longer led a group of pack horses in local parades, Ernie rode "shotgun" on a horse-pulled antique wagon, always with one of Uncle Pete's guns in full view across his lap.

Uncle Fred's wife, Nettie Anderson Wetle, served homemade bread that Ernie consumed with gusto. Aunt Nettie's cookie jar contained delicious treats and her dinner table was laden with tasty fresh foods from the ample vegetable garden. Ernie's palate welcomed exposure to well-prepared fresh foods. His mother was also a good cook, but she went to the market for her produce instead of to the garden.

Ernie rode all over the Chenowith area with his uncles and Grandpa Anderson when they hunted coyotes or other varmints. His love of hunting lasted throughout his lifetime. He became acquainted with knapweed, bindweed, scrub oak, and the tall fir and pine trees scattered over the area's ridges, valleys, and rolling hills. As a youngster, he lost a gold pocket watch above Chenowith, on Government Flat. Although he scoured that piece of geography carefully over the years and eventually owned it, he never found his watch.

Ernie was devoted to his parents. He helped at the shop and observed his dad's methods and work habits. His father wanted everything "done right so it will last," and he wanted the store and the work area to be tidy. He strove to be thorough in his work by finishing a specific task and cleaning up before tackling another project. Ernie grew up embracing his dad's work ethic and also his respect for the people who operated his farm holdings.

Young Ernie accompanied his dad as often as he could when he went to visit the ranch on the breaks of the Deschutes, leased from Henry by George Wagenblast. Ernie learned all the routes to get there and back, and at times delivered messages or supplies for his father.

Henry also had acreage located on the Klickitat Hills in Washington, across the Columbia River. On one occasion, when Ernie was a teenager, Henry sent his son to the ranch on an errand. The boy saddled up, crossed on the ferry, and rode to the ranch. Since it was a nice, sunny day, Ernie and the hired man decided to go coyote hunting, which gave Ernie a late start returning

Young Ernie

Courtesy of Columbia Gorge Discovery Center

Ernie's Beginnings

home. He did not realize that the ferry stopped running at sundown until he arrived at the dock at dusk. Fortunately, the ferry maintained stables for its patrons to use. Ernie decided not to ride the long distance back to the ranch; he bedded down his horse in one of the stalls and made a bed for himself in another. After a good night's rest, Ernie returned home, where his mother greeted him with a few well-chosen words.

As a youngster, Ernie knew the Ketchum family, who owned a ranch in the Chenowith creek area. These days, it can be identified as "just beyond the Chenowith Airpark," but Ernie knew it as being located out Chenowith Road before you get to Doyle Grade. The Ketchums owned some Black Angus cattle, but their principal interest was in a large flock of sheep. Ernie warmed to the lambs and, as soon as he was old enough, began helping Mr. Ketchum. They became fast friends—such good friends that in later years, their relationship survived Ernie's repeated effort to purchase property and/or rights-of-way from the Ketchum spread.

Bill Ketchum hired Ernie to herd sheep during school vacations. The pay was one dollar a day, and he slept under the stars. Ernie loved it. One Friday evening, he prevailed on his dad to take him in the family car, a big, air-cooled Franklin, to the end of the pavement so he could hike on up to the sheep camp. He described that walk about sixty-five years later in vivid detail, recalling, "I was a little guy, but I could always carry as much stuff as anyone in a backpack." The full moon and soft light made for a dreamlike walk. This appears to be one of those times that he yearned to get out of town.

Ernie told about an occasion when the Ketchums needed his help to bring sheep in from summer grazing. One of the herders had a little problem. He had gone to town and come back "seein' snakes." The man with the hangover thought he was going to die and insisted that they get a priest for him. Dealing with him caused the Ketchums to get a late start. Bad weather was threatening but they had to bring the flock home before winter snows fell. They managed to ford several creeks with the animals before the storm broke in a veritable cloudburst. They were caught with just one more creek to cross as the water rose. As Ernie recalled, twelve or fifteen sheep became waterlogged and drowned in the rushing waters.

He said, "Guess who got to stay back, skin out the dead animals, and bring in the pelts?" In the cold, wet weather, Ernie salvaged the pelts and made his way home. Asked about overtime, he replied, "In sheep camp, a work day is twenty-four hours."

Ernie's older brother, Harry, enjoyed the socially accepted youth activities of his day. Professionally, Harry became a newspaper editor in Pendleton, Oregon, and later lived in California. While Ernie enjoyed getting out of town, he was also active in school. The Dalles High School *Steelhead* reveals that he took the "commercial course" and was also vice president of the junior class, on the executive committee of the Literary Society, and senior basketball captain.

Apparently each class selected a basketball team to play interclass competition. As captain, Ernie led the seniors to win the school championship. The faculty selected Ernie as one of the five all-star basketball players of the class, noting: "The forwards, Ernest Kuck and Elmore Hill, are small but fast and both are accurate basket shooters. These two forwards work systematically together."

CHAPTER 2

Screaming Meemies and the Grub Hoe

Ernie graduated from The Dalles High School in 1916. On May 25, 1917, he enlisted in the army in Troop D, First Oregon Cavalry unit, at Pendleton, Oregon. He immediately applied for and received permission to be in The Dalles on his twenty-first birthday, July 29, when he would be eligible to become a member of the Elks. His friends said that he did not expect to return from the war, so if the worst happened, he wanted his name on the roles of The Dalles Elks Lodge.

On November 17, 1917, the military disbanded Ernie's cavalry unit and transferred the troops to Battery B, 148th Field Artillery. They departed from New York on January 22, 1918, to serve in France and Germany under General John J. Pershing. The young soldiers received basic training, but when Ernie entered his first offensive action as a truck driver transporting supplies to the front, he felt totally unprepared. He participated in the Champagne-Marne Defensive and the Aisne-Marne Offensive in July/August, 1918.

During that summer, Colonel William "Billy" Mitchell introduced 1,476 airplanes to be used for "observation, pursuit and bombardment" to help counter the 500 planes the Germans were using. The Allies' First Air Service had

Ernie Kuck, World War I

Courtesy of Columbia Gorge Discovery Center

been formed from limited resources using planes from other countries and inexperienced soldiers and pilots. That air service would soon replace the horse cavalry as the eyes and ears of the army.

On September 26, 1918, Ernie Kuck, still a truck driver assigned to Mitchell's unit, most probably helped move the men and their gear the sixty miles for the next planned action—the Meuse-Argonne Offensive. They were ultimately successful, but 26,277 troops died and 95,786 were injured, making it the largest and bloodiest operation of the war for the American Expeditionary Force.

After that decisive battle, the Germans surrendered their unit. General Pershing, however, refused to accept their surrender until the entire German army had surrendered. He pushed his two armies to attack without mercy. The war ended on November 11, 1918.

Ernie had survived the vicious engagements of the military. He remained in Germany as part of the occupation, but petitioned for a transfer to France to enroll in school until his orders came through to return stateside. Ernie arrived back in the United States on June 15, 1919, and travelled to Camp Lewis at American Lake, Washington (later known as Fort Lewis).

On June 27, Ernie tucked the honorable discharge from the Expeditionary Forces safely in his wallet and rode the train to Portland. There he changed trains and settled in for the last lap of his long journey home.

He felt his luggage to be sure that he still had the short-handled pick that had been government-issued to the artillery. Ernie had used it well and often to dig fox holes in Europe for his protection when the noisy German artillery shells whizzed by. The "screaming meemies," as they were called, unnerved the best of soldiers. Ernie opted to bring that useful little tool home, where it became a permanent fixture in his pick-up truck. Ernie hated knapweed, and that little "grub hoe" was always handy to eradicate those noxious plants.

Peering out the window of the train, he let his thoughts drift ahead to his destination. The conductor's resonant call, "All aboard!" interrupted his pondering. The train started to move slowly and evenly as it passed over the railroad bridge and turned, entering the plains east of Portland, before it came to the ruggedly beautiful formations of the Columbia River Gorge. Ernie enjoyed looking out the train window, but the scenery did not rouse the strong feelings of "home" that he would experience when he arrived in Wasco County, where he knew the terrain so well from hours of riding his horse over the hills.

As he returned to his memories, he could visualize the tastefully furnished, comfortable home where his mother graciously made guests feel welcome. He wondered what she would be wearing; whatever it was, it would be covered with a crisp, freshly ironed apron while she worked in the kitchen. It would be great to see her again. How he had missed her cooking while in the army. He imagined he could smell the food already!

He glanced out the window and recognized the little town of Troutdale before the tracks crossed the Sandy River and continued east to the basalt rock formations in the Gorge. The train travelled so close to the south bank of the Columbia River that most of the waterfalls cascading down were only in sight near the river level. He didn't know the names of all of them, but Multnomah Falls was unmistakable. He remembered it was the second highest falls in the United States. He had looked up the actual height, which was 620 feet. He leaned forward and looked upward out the window so he could see the elevated bridge constructed between the upper and lower falls. Multnomah Falls originated from basalt formations further south than most, so he could see it more easily.

Upriver on the north bank, Beacon Rock appeared on the horizon. Ernie had officially entered the Gorge. As he observed additional waterfalls and huge basaltic rock formations, he slipped back into memories.

He thought about having his own room—all to himself. He wondered what new project his dad would be promoting. His father enjoyed people and actively participated in the community. He was a longtime volunteer fireman, helped organize and was a stockholder in the Citizens National Bank of The Dalles, and assisted Hotel Dalles with his business acumen.

As a devoted member of the Elks Lodge, Henry served as Exalted Ruler in 1903–1904. Local politics also captured his interest; he served as a councilman and mayor of the city of The Dalles and chaired the Wasco County Republican Central Committee. Yes, Ernie's dad kept busy with one thing or another. Wondering what his father would do next, Ernie watched the spectacular rock formations, noting the detail on some of the stone guardrails along the "daylight" edge of the new Scenic Columbia River Highway.

He made mental note of passing Cascade Locks, the halfway point between Portland and The Dalles. The train continued east, hugging close to the river's edge as it snaked through the narrow gorge. The landscape appeared more familiar as the train slowed at Hood River; the routine stop seemed interminable to the impatient young ex-soldier.

Ernie watched a ferry approaching the Oregon shore as he pondered what he would find to do in The Dalles. He had helped at the leather shop and knew how to work with leather, but when enlisting in the military, he had listed his occupation as bookkeeper. Perhaps he could continue bookkeeping and take care of purchasing supplies and inventory too. But he'd rather be outside. He thought of his dad's wheat ranch on the Deschutes—maybe he could lease that—but he'd rather work with cattle than farm.

Finally the train pulled out of the Hood River station. He was very familiar with the next area—his back yard! He knew every inch of the top of the Mosier countryside. From the train, he could see the northern face of the hills as they dropped down to meet the waters of the Columbia. Remembering his rides on the top of those steep formations, he could almost feel the breeze in his face.

The train moved on past the little cluster of houses at Rowena. As the Klickitat Mountains on the north shore came into view, Ernie recalled the seasonal changes: from the green grass of spring to the now beautiful golden sheen of summer that would become the muted earth tones of fall until one morning the mountains would be dusted with snow—a sure sign of approaching winter.

As the train neared Crates Point, the rails curved in a south-southeast direction following the south bank of the Columbia. From the left side of the train, Ernie could see his hometown at last—a crescent of buildings that hugged the big bend in the river. He noted the tall pines on the top of Sorosis and the steep drop to the residential area covering the hillside down to the commercial district. He couldn't see his home, but he knew it was right below the hospital. The broad

Screaming Meemies and the Grub Hoe

expanse of white paint on the front of that particular building stood out as an unmistakable landmark. The Catholic Church spire with the six-foot-tall rooster on top still dominated the west edge of town.

The train slowed. It crossed the trestle over the Mill Creek delta and came to a full stop at the depot. Ernie checked his luggage again to be sure he still had the little grub hoe. When he enlisted and left for World War I, he had never expected to see The Dalles again. Now, here he was—home—with his whole life ahead of him.

Helen Huntington Kuck

Photo from author's personal files

CHAPTER 3

Ernie's First Love

Local boys returned from World War I ready to enjoy small-town activities. While Ernie had been in the service for two years, Helen Huntington had attended the University of Oregon. They each returned to The Dalles and inevitably perceived it and each other in a new light. That Ernie and Helen started dating seemed meant to be. They had attended the same schools, the same church, and they both danced, played cards, and enjoyed parties.

    Helen, the youngest of six children, lost her father in 1900 when she was three years old. Graduating from The Dalles High School in 1915, Helen worked locally until her brother, Charles (called "Shy") was selected as University of Oregon football coach in 1918. As faculty, he could not live in his fraternity (Phi Delta Theta), so he prevailed on his mother, Mary Huntington, to sell her house in The Dalles and move to Eugene. The family lived together and Helen enrolled in the university. She joined the Kappa Kappa Gamma Sorority but resided at her mother's home. When Shy married two years later, Mary and Helen returned to The Dalles and rented an apartment. Helen went to work at the bank.

Helen weighed a little less than 100 pounds and was less than five feet tall. She always wore dainty high-heeled shoes to appear a little taller. She was pretty, with lots of dark hair marcelled in perfect waves with never a stray lock, and she dressed elegantly.

Service records indicate Ernie was 5'6" tall when he joined the army in 1917. Ernie's genteel upbringing had prepared him for formal events. He had a tuxedo and patent leather shoes for such social occasions, although he was not gregarious.

The Kuck and Huntington families knew each other from church but, as the relationship between Ernie and Helen developed, it became apparent that Helen's mother did not approve of this particular young man as a son-in-law. She had aspirations for her daughter to marry a professional man who would provide a large home so that Helen could entertain other professional couples. In Mary's eyes, the lack of a suit and tie for work clothes overshadowed Ernie's positive traits. She resented the fact that he was the son of a harness maker and not the son of a doctor or lawyer—a "professional man."

When Ernie dressed for work he wore boots with jeans and a kerchief around his neck. Sometimes, at the end of the day, his clothing exuded a barnyard fragrance—not particularly pleasant for the Huntingtons, who stayed away from ranches and didn't tramp around pastures or take part in trail rides.

For these reasons, Mary was unalterably opposed to her youngest and most-beloved child marrying Ernie Kuck. Her outspoken negativity and dominant demeanor grew more shrill as the wedding date neared. Her children were actually afraid that she might suffer a nervous breakdown.

In spite of all this stress, Ernie and Helen were married on April 8, 1922. The ceremony took place at the Congregational

Church in a simple, late afternoon service conducted by family friend and former minister at The Dalles, the Reverend Daniel Poling. The local paper reported that Helen wore a dark blue tailleur, a blue hat, and a corsage of Cecile Brunner roses. The couple did not have a reception, but left immediately for the Seattle area for an extended wedding trip. They returned to The Dalles to the home they had rented at 610 Court Street.

Mary's older daughter, Hazel, married to Allie Gronewald, invited her mother to live with them while Helen and Ernie honeymooned. The Gronewalds had a three-year-old son, Jerrold, who helped divert the thoughts of the grieving grandma. As Jerrold learned to talk, his attempt to say *Grandmother* sounded like *Ammer*—and so Mary's name became Ammer. Her whole family, the grandchildren, the neighbors, and the clerks at the little neighborhood store all called her "Ammer." Hazel was eight months pregnant, and Ammer helped in the household. She felt needed, which helped assuage her grief.

In 1924, Ernie and Helen settled into their own home at 1210 Jackson Street (now East Ninth Street) in anticipation of their first child. Interestingly, the house they bought had the same basic layout as their rented house, except that the new home included a basement, a garage, and a fireplace with a mantel on one side of the living room. It also had a big back yard.

The mother-daughter bond between Ammer and Helen was so firmly established that soon Ammer gave up her apartment and settled into the larger front bedroom in Ernie and Helen's house. With a baby arriving soon, Helen would need extra help. However, Ammer's opinion of Ernie had not changed.

Ernie didn't argue. If offended, he acted as though the opponent had vanished from the face of the earth. When angry, his face would get red, his mouth would become tight, and he would turn and walk away.

Helen found herself living with two people she loved who failed to communicate with each other. This difficult position took its toll on her health. Some people perceived Helen as an invalid; others thought her a hypochondriac. No doubt she suffered greatly from the constant tension in her home.

CHAPTER 4

Jimmy

Everyone rejoiced on August 2, 1924, when Ernie and Helen's baby boy arrived. It was decision time: what to name him? Everyone liked his grandfather, Henry Kuck. They had also admired Helen's father, the deceased James Huntington. Ernie and Helen chose to call him "James Henry." Ammer had made it known that she preferred boys, and welcomed this new grandson. Of course, every father wants a son, and every mother's firstborn is unique and very special to her. Little Jimmy immediately occupied center stage in the home.

As a baby, little Jimmy was not Ernie's responsibility. Once out of diapers, though, he eased into being a daddy's boy and spent lots of time at the ranch. When Jimmy learned to ride, Ernie bought him a cute little piebald pony named "Maggie." Ernie's ranch hands welcomed Jimmy into their activities and helped him learn his way around the stock.

Although Ammer's presence created tension at home, she often took care of Jimmy when Ernie and Helen went together to a card party or social event. Helen disdained Ernie's livestock; she never rode horses, not even to enjoy the beautiful moonlight trail rides he arranged. Jimmy spent time with Daddy at the ranch or at home with Mom and Ammer.

Ernie, Jimmy, and Helen Kuck

Jimmy with his maternal grandmother,
Mary Huntington, a.k.a. Ammer

These strained relationships exerted a serious impact on family activities.

Ernie often stopped to visit his parents at his childhood home. He admired his father and emulated his principles. H. L. Kuck invested time, energy, and money in helping good things happen in The Dalles. He was also a state legislator, and the community keenly felt the loss when he died after a stroke in 1935.

Losing a father who had been a valued counselor created a devastating void in Ernie's life. He spent more time in the beautiful forested mountains with his horse and cattle. The sound of birds calling, squirrels scampering, the breeze in the tall trees, or the thrashing of branches in a strong wind, all accompanied by the sound of cowbells worn by cattle scattered far and wide, soothed Ernie's troubled spirit. He adopted the mountains as his haven from sadness and stress.

While grieving over the loss of his father, Jimmy's youth and vitality offered Ernie solace. The boy was a good student and active in school and sports. He also enjoyed swimming in the new natatorium in The Dalles. During the summer, when not at the ranch, he often prevailed upon his mother to take him to the "nat" to swim.

The summer before he entered high school, Jimmy had outgrown another set of clothes, including his cowboy boots. Ernie gave Jimmy a new pair in July as an early present for his fifteenth birthday. He wore the stiff new boots without breaking them in and came home from the ranch with a blister.

It was a small blister and it didn't really hurt. To find relief from the summer heat, Jimmy went swimming at the nat. The blister didn't heal as they expected. It became red and swollen. Jimmy developed a temperature and went to the doctor, who

Jimmy with a young bear   Jim at 14

Photos from author's personal files

Jimmy

expressed concern and admitted him to the hospital. The old hospital building had no air conditioning—only a few fans and a wimpy breeze in the evening to relieve the stifling heat. The temperature soared.

Several days later, the blister seemed better and the boy's family hoped for a speedy recovery. Then another lesion appeared on Jimmy's knee, resulting in more pain and fever, followed by more treatment, poultices, and packs. The infection moved to the mastoid area and within days, young Jimmy had passed away. Three adults had suddenly lost their reason for living. Dark days ahead brought deep, unrelenting sadness to all of them.

Jimmy's death was a terrible blow to Ernie. He later confided to friend Carol Daniels that Ammer blamed the new boots and, by extension, Ernie. There was enough blame to go around, for if Jimmy had been kept away from swimming when he had a blister, he might not have contracted the streptococcus infection that killed him. There was no effective treatment for strep in 1939.

The women attempted to console each other, but they seemed unable to find any comfort. According to the custom of the day, they went to the mortuary to view the beautifully prepared body. Ammer had lost her purposeful walk and entered the viewing room with a hesitant shuffle. As she approached the casket, her face brightened a little. She turned to Helen and said, "Oh, look, he is just asleep." As she reached out to touch him, she recoiled from the cold hand. Her body sagged as she realized that Jimmy was really lost to them.

Jimmy's death marked the beginning of Ammer's mental and physical deterioration. She moved in with Hazel, who had returned to teaching when she was widowed in 1929. In the fall, Hazel hired a woman to stay with Ammer during the day. Eventually, Ammer wandered from home in spite of the caregiver's efforts to restrain her. It was finally decided that this sad old woman should move to Portland to live with her son, Walter, and his family. Unfortunately, even there she appeared frequently in their living room with her coat on and her bags packed "to go someplace else to live—the kids are too noisy—the family is too busy." Eventually, Walter found an appropriate care center and engaged a room for her. The next time her bags appeared in the living room, he asked, "Should we go for a ride and see if we can find a place you would like?" She readily agreed. When they arrived at the care center, the staff greeted her as a potential resident. When shown a room, she decided she wanted to stay and she lived the rest of her days in that excellent facility.

Helen's chronic ill health and grief interfered with her daily living skills. Ernie hired someone to do light housekeeping and most of the cooking. He shifted his daily activities so that he could give more time to Helen while still looking after his stock and visiting his mother every day, as well as meeting his responsibilities at the store.

To cope with the loss of his son, Ernie spent increasing amounts of time in the mountains riding his favorite horse. He needed that solitary time on the hills, where he could revel in the unimpeded views of Mt. Hood and Mt. Adams, accompanied by the whisper of wind and the muted sound of cow bells in the timber.

His friends shared his sadness, but words could not ease the deep pain or the loss that Ernie felt. When they saw him, they would greet him and give him an opportunity to visit. But when he rode off toward the pasture, they understood his need to be alone and their sympathy followed him.

Jimmy

Then Minnie Anderson Kuck, Ernie's mother, died suddenly of an acute asthma attack on November 7, 1943, at the age of 74. Helen helped as much as she was able, organizing personal effects and getting the old family house ready for sale.

Helen's mother, Ammer, continued to deteriorate, and died peacefully on December 9, 1945. Her children made funeral arrangements, including burial in the family plot at the IOOF Cemetery in The Dalles. The entire family gathered for the services except for Helen, who had been admitted to the hospital on her doctor's recommendation. Three of Helen's siblings visited her there after the funeral.

Following Jimmy's death, Helen endured six heartbroken and inconsolable years; she passed away two weeks after her mother died. The family gathered again for her services, saddened by her early demise and full of sympathy for Ernie, who was now truly all alone. Within ten short years, he had lost both parents, his son, his mother-in-law, and his wife; his whole world had changed.

He spent time at the Elks Lodge. He never missed an Elks meeting; he also spent quite a bit of time at the club during the week. Even people who did not know him well identified him as "the quiet little man who reads while sitting in one of the big red leather chairs in the Elks lobby."

Ernie returned to his haven among the trees. Friends saw him coming and going—always alone. They agreed, "Ernie is a loner." Deep loss and stress intensified this. He spent more time in the hills at the line cabins. Ernie always said, "It pays to have an extra bale of hay for stock and extra wood for the fire." These cabins provided food, fuel, and shelter for men and horses, both for the gathering-in season and as a refuge in bad weather. Now they provided Ernie with a quiet place where he could stay for days at a time, finding a way to accept the painful realities of his world.

He had cattle to tend and move to different pasture. He checked the water supply for his stock and supervised logging contracts when necessary. Eventually, the comfortable routine of these activities eased him back into the lives of other cattlemen. He spent time with his Uncle Fred and Aunt Nettie Wetle, the only family that remained to him.

Friend Elden Wagenblast returned from serving in World War II and upon seeing Ernie downtown, would ask, "How're you feeling today?" For a long time, Ernie answered "Rough," and Elden would simply say, "Good-bye, I'll see you later." But eventually, Ernie said, "Rough" followed with a grin, and Elden knew he was ready to talk.

CHAPTER 5

Another Ernie

While grieving the loss of his family, Ernie made acquaintance with a newcomer to The Dalles, Ernie Rhodes. Rhodes had not known Jimmy, Ernie's parents, or Helen. His friendship would be a healing balm for Ernie Kuck's aching heart.

Ernie Rhodes arrived in The Dalles in 1943, just in time to watch Ernie's spring cattle drive pass through town. He thought to himself, "I don't know who is doing that, but I'll find out, and when they do it again, I'm going to be part of it." He belonged to a farmers' association called the Grange, and when he transferred his membership to Chenowith, the fates smiled on him. He met the Wetles, and they arranged for him to ride in their nephew's cattle drive the following year. He didn't get really acquainted with Ernie Kuck for many months, though.

During the week, Rhodes managed the Chenowith Irrigation District, but he offered to ride with Ernie on weekends if there was stock to be moved. The very next week, he received a call from Ernie. In his characteristically brief manner, Ernie said he would be down to get Rhodes and his horse at seven o'clock on Saturday. Rhodes tells the story:

Seven o'clock he was down there with his little truck. We loaded my horse up and there we went. He was taking a bunch of cattle—must have been twenty-five or thirty head—down to Mosier Creek. He was on what we call the Ketchum Road now. He didn't tell me where he was taking the herd. So up the road we went. He started the cows down my way and I kept pushing them up onto the road. He was on one side of them and I was on the other. Pretty soon he yelled at me, "Get back!" That was the only thing he said.

I said, "Why didn't you tell me you were going down there into Mosier Creek?"

"Guess I lost my voice."

Those were the only words he said. We got into the timber down there and, come noon, I unsaddled. My horse was lathered—it was a warm day and my horse was soft [not in shape]. I took the saddle off of her, so the air could get to her back. Ernie watched me all the time I was doing it. He loosened his own saddle. We sat down and had a drink out of the creek. I don't know where we took the cattle, but we followed them all afternoon. They seemed to know where they were going. We got over there and turned them loose. It was just about dusk when we got back to the Phirman place, and he loaded me and my horse into his truck and brought us home. Never said "Thank you" or nothin'. Just, "I guess we're all done for the day."

Well, I think now, remembering that day, that my little horse was just dripping wet with sweat at noontime. I think Ernie kind of admired it that I had unsaddled her and rubbed her down and let the air get to her back.

Another Ernie

That was what I figured out later—that he judged you by the way you took care of your animals. Because he really took care of his own and he expected somebody else to do the same thing.

Ernie liked people. He didn't have much to say, but he liked to have somebody around him once in a while. You never saw him to a saddle club meeting but, if they had an event, he was there, as a usual rule. He went to the festivities and celebrations, and he'd sit there with that little grin on his face.

Rhodes had come into Ernie Kuck's life at a time when Ernie needed a friend who would not remind him of activities involving Jimmy. They had started their relationship on a clean slate, looking forward to things they each enjoyed.

The front window of Kuck & Bonney Sporting Goods

Courtesy of Columbia Gorge Discovery Center

CHAPTER 6

Kuck & Bonney Sporting Goods

Ernie's father, Henry L. Kuck, was born in 1862, the son of a harness and saddle maker in Lansing, Iowa. After school he spent five years in Minneapolis mastering his father's trade, and then headed west in 1886. He first established a shop in Shaniko, Oregon, and then moved to The Dalles in 1889. His shop there, along with the Eureka Restaurant and Skibbe Saloon, were destroyed in a major fire in 1891. Henry started over but suffered a second devastating loss in 1894 when the Columbia River flooded, cresting at the highest mark ever recorded, fifty-nine feet. He salvaged a few tools and started again.

Ralph Bonney moved to The Dalles from Echo, Oregon, in 1911 and opened a livery stable. He, too, had completed a full apprenticeship in leather work. Henry preferred to make harnesses, and it was not long before he had hired Ralph, who specialized in saddles. Together they developed a thriving business.

Ernie worked at the shop as a lad, and kept the books prior to his military service. Shortly after returning from Europe, he joined the business; the name changed to Kuck & Son, Sporting Goods on July 1, 1919. Perhaps the demand for reins and harnesses had diminished with the advent of the automobile, or maybe Henry was just pleased with the way Ralph and Ernie were minding the store, because he chose to retire in 1922. Henry sold his half interest to Ralph Bonney and the business name changed again, becoming Kuck & Bonney Sporting Goods—but this time *Kuck* referred to Ernest, not his father. For many years, Kuck & Bonney saddles were recognized throughout eastern Oregon for their excellent quality.

Although Ernie could do leather work, he chose not to. Ralph frequently bought needed supplies and Ernie paid the bills when they came in. Ernie didn't need to be at the store all the time, but customers didn't keep bankers hours and sometimes needed things early in the morning or late in the day to be ready for work the next morning. Ralph came to work about seven in the morning and the shop closed at six in the evening—eleven hours a day, six days a week.

A number of longtime residents of The Dalles related happy memories from times spent in Ernie and Ralph's harness shop. It provided a meeting place for families to gather before the trip home to outlying ranches and homesteads. Children were welcome to wander in, look at the displays, and wait patiently with the group around the stove until their parents came.

The shop building, an unimposing, big corrugated metal box without insulation, filled the corner lot. Before Ernie's father opened the harness shop, the building had been occupied by the Stubling Liquor Store. Ralph Bonney described the building as "hot in the summer, cold in the winter, and noisy when it rained."

As a boy, Ernie's friend Mannie Wasson loved to visit the shop. He would pause to look at the interesting stuff in the windows on either side of the big front door. Then he would step inside, take a deep breath, and savor the smell of leather.

Young Mannie eagerly viewed the gleaming glass display cases that held many enticing items neatly arranged. The showcases extended the length of the room one on each side and one down the middle. As he looked at the stack of colorful saddle blankets, he couldn't help but dream a little. He couldn't remember when he didn't have his own horse. He liked to ride and he looked forward to a time when he would have his own ranch. There were so many saddles that it took a long time to admire them all—the big ones, the little ones, the working saddles, the show saddles—each one unique. He timidly fingered the tooling of his dream saddle.

The bridles and harnesses hung from hooks in the rafters. There were many kinds, each for a special purpose. Bridles for saddle horses had reins, but the sturdier, heavy reins, called lines, were used to guide teams of work horses. Slender, lighter lines were made for horses pulling buggies in town. Some of the harnesses had bells attached.

Ernie's neighbor, Helen Sallee, remembered team bells that she used on the leaders of her team of six or eight horses. The bells hung from the angora goatskin cover on the hame (a piece of the harness that goes across the lead pair and connects the whole team to the vehicle). Most of the roads in the countryside were narrow, with few places for teams to pass. When a driver heard oncoming bells, he looked for a wide place by the side of the road to wait for the other team to come into view. Drivers also believed that bells on the teams kept the horses more or less in step.

Mannie could almost hear the bells as he thought of them. The tents and tarps didn't interest the young lad yet, but the pocket knives and small hatchets surely did! Then he came to a beautiful display of cow bells. Bigger than the little bells used on harnesses, these sturdy bells could survive trips into thick brush. As he viewed a rectangular bell about eight inches long, he wished he could hear it. He restrained his impulse to pick it up and ring it, as that would really get everyone's attention! He saw square bells, oblong bells, round bells, and a few that were actually bell-shaped.

He remembered searching for cows himself; and at times, although he heard the sound of the bell, he was unable to follow it to find the lost animal. Cattle on the open range would follow the best grazing as they wandered, often scattering long distances over the hills by roundup time. Occasionally a cow in thick brush would become invisible, but the bell could usually be heard. Riding into thickets made a cowboy really appreciate his leather chaps.

Mannie could remember hearing the Nagle sisters (Helen, Florence, and May) talking about the cowbells. They had one that their folks had brought with them from Illinois when they came to Oregon in 1878. They used that on a cow for about twelve years. They called her "Old Swiss Bell" and, as far as they knew, the bell still had its original clapper. They used it until 1940, then put it into their collection of treasures. They could hear that particular bell for miles, but could never tell where the sound was coming from!

On the wall behind the counter hung a row of straps that would hold a bell around a cow's neck. These straps measured about two inches wide and about forty inches long, with a conventional belt buckle on one end. The bell straps, made from the part of the hide that had covered an animal's back, didn't stretch like hide from the rest of the animal.

Kuck & Bonney Sporting Goods

Retail space occupied the front two-thirds of the fifty-foot-long building. A door in the center of the back wall provided access to the workroom and Ernie's office. Mannie usually heard laughter coming from that back room, so he drifted toward chairs circling the pot-bellied stove that seemed to invite folks to gather 'round and hear the latest news. Soon, the fellowship shared by the men enveloped him, and he felt as if he belonged there. Often folks meandered into the workroom to wait for family or chat with Ralph Bonney and watch as he continued with his saddle work. Ralph was eventually joined in the shop by his son, Garth. In this back room, near the office, stood a massive black floor safe with "W.B. Wilshire & Co." emblazoned on the door. Above the door in bold capitals was "HENRY L. KUCK." (The safe is currently located in the Baldwin Saloon on First and Court Streets in The Dalles.)

In the main workroom, belts came down from the ceiling, connecting the drive shaft above to the various machines in the shop. A worktable—large enough to spread out a whole hide for cutting—filled the space near the back wall, where tools and accessories were kept within easy reach. The warmed wax the craftsmen used on their "thread" was always in a convenient spot. The fragrant odor of fresh leather filled the entire store, blending with the singular odor of the rawhide gloves made by local Indians—a unique, unforgettable smell.

From Ernie's elevated office in the corner of the shop, he could watch through a large window for customers in the store who needed help. A double door opened into the workroom from the Laughlin Street side near the alley. The Kuck family lived a block and a half away and this was the closest door to home for them. Merchandise was also delivered to this side door.

As Mannie grew up, he continued to enjoy visits to Kuck & Bonney's, and the displays prompted more dreams, more wishes. At the age of seventeen, he approached the shop with a purposeful step, for he had the cash in his pocket to buy his heart's desire. He knew just which pair of boots he wanted and as he paid for them, it seemed that the door had opened to his future. He left the shop a happy young man.

The shop attracted other young men who liked the smell of fresh leather and appreciated the practical items on display in the gleaming showcases. Viewing the merchandise inspired youngsters and young men to work for their dreamed-for equipment. One of them was Joe Miller, who offered these colorful reminiscences:

> I was probably in my early teens and I was at the store and Ernie asked me if I was going to ride in the parade. I sez, "No, I don't have no saddle."
>
> "Ya still got old Lady, the white horse?"
>
> "Yeah."
>
> "I'm going to ride my horse and lead two pack horses in the parade on the Fourth of July. I got a saddle for you if you want to ride in the parade."
>
> "Ya have?"
>
> "Yeah . . . It was Jimmy's saddle."
>
> It was the first time anybody ever rode that saddle after Jimmy died in '39. And he let me use it!
>
> I had Lady there at the Saddle Shop early on July 4. 'Ernie saddled my horse and I was soon on her back and ready to go. Ernie had a final word—"Now you follow me in the parade."

"I will."

When the parade ended, I told him, "I'll take the saddle and blanket back to the shop."

Ernie's answer was stern and short: "No. You aren't going to ride bareback way out there to Five Mile where you live."

I thought, "Well, I rode bareback comin' in!" We didn't have no way to truck our horses at all. We had to ride 'em. You didn't argue with Ernie, so I rode home on Jimmy's saddle. I forget now whether he said "next day" or "when yer dad comes in, just bring the saddle and blanket." I already had the bridle that I used and he loaned me the saddle and blanket . . . Jimmy's saddle and blanket.

Another day Joe, as a teenager, was in the saddle shop looking. Just looking. He returned to the saddle display frequently. Ernie was in his office, watching Joe through the window. Eventually, Ernie came out to talk to the young man and Joe recalls the conversation as follows:

Ernie sez, "Well, so you like 'em?"

"I like 'em all, but I don't have no money."

"Well, when are you going to get some money?"

"When I sell my two steers this fall, I'll have the money."

"Ya got a saddle picked out?"

I made two or three trips down the row of saddles—there were about eight there. "Yeah, I like this saddle . . . but I still don't have no money."

"I didn't ask if you had any money." Ernie got the saddle and he set it on a saddle horse and sez, "Come up front with me." There was a big rack of saddle blankets. "Now, a fellow with a new saddle's gotta have a new saddle blanket," sez Ernie.

"I can't afford that."

"Oh, yeah, yeah . . . That's gotta go with a new saddle."

So I picked the saddle blanket out and he got his long pole with the hook on it to reach the bridles, all hanging from the rafters. He took down about three of them.

"OK . . . pick out your bridle."

I think I picked the third one. He took it into the office and put my name on it and the next day, my dad went in with the truck and picked it up. Never signed a paper—nuthin'. That was about—oh, let's see—haying time in June. In October or November, I sold my two steers. Ernie didn't charge me interest nor nothin'. I never signed my John Henry nor nothin'. I sold my two steers along with my dad's other steers and went in and paid Ernie $103–I don't remember if that covered the saddle or everything. Bonney had made the saddle, and it was a good one.

CHAPTER 7

Mutual Respect

Author's note: I am well aware that at this time, it is politically correct to call the first settlers on the American continent "Native Americans." But in Ernie's day, they were called "Indians." For authenticity, I use that old-fashioned term. If you had called them Native Americans, people in those days would have said, "Who?"

One day, Elden Wagenblast and his dad walked past the Indians that often squatted in front of the saddle shop with their backs to the display windows. As father and son stepped inside, they walked to the back room and noticed some Indians sitting on one side of the room and Ernie sitting on the other. Elden was curious because quiet filled the room—only a little monosyllable was heard once in a while, sometimes from Indians, and sometimes from Ernie. He watched them and finally asked his dad if they were mad at each other. Dad said the Indians were selling Ernie some horses. The saddle shop didn't deal in horses, but sometimes Ernie bought for himself, or for someone else who couldn't communicate with the Indians. He seemed to understand the Indians and they respected him. He respected them, too, and always dealt fairly with them.

Ernie kept handmade rawhide gloves in stock. He bought them from the Indian women at Simnasho, who tanned the hides and made the gloves just as their tribe had done for years before them. These gloves exuded a very unique smell! Ernie always wore rawhide gloves when working with his horses or cattle. Neighbor Bob Sallee recalled that "Whenever it rained, you always knew where Kuck was. You could smell those gloves a mile away!"

Ernie helped the Indian women find the hides. They tanned them, made the gloves, and the shop bought them. It went on the "books." This gave the mothers a resource with which to supply their families with necessities, and it kept cash out of the hands of the bootleggers.

The store also carried beautiful beadwork bags made by the women and saddle cinches made from the hair of cows' tails. Ernie supplied the "D" rings, and the Indians brought the cinches back for him to sell in the store.

The Indian women and Ernie apparently never haggled over money because he dealt fairly and they trusted him. Whenever they came in to make a payment, they would say "half on my bill." If they only gave him ten dollars, he still credited their account properly whether they owed him fifteen dollars or fifty dollars. The "paying half" was a figure of speech, and Ernie kept impeccable records.

As Ernie's father watched automobiles grow in popularity, he expressed his concern to Ernie that if horses and buggies became obsolete, business might slack off. Ernie convinced his dad that they should cater to the Indian business, because Indians would be the last to give up their horses. While not fully convinced, H. L. agreed and encouraged Ernie to continue to deal with them. Eventually the need for harnesses did diminish, but the waiting list for Kuck & Bonney saddles grew.

For twenty-five years, Garth Bonney (Ralph's son) donated a saddle to the Fort Dalles Rodeo annually as an award to the "All-Around" winner. Even after his retirement, Garth continued making saddles. When asked why he made another saddle for the rodeo champion, he answered in his quiet way, "I guess I just got homesick for the leather." He donated one additional rodeo saddle, his last, in 1994—fifty years after his father, Ralph Boney, had become a partner in Kuck & Bonney.

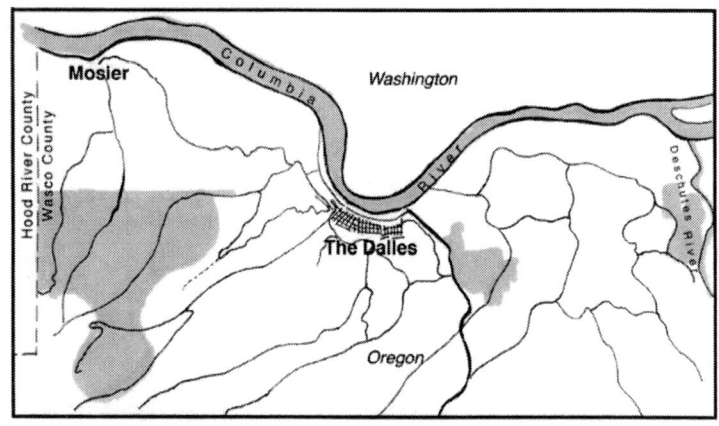

Map created by Irene Hill. Kuck property boundaries (shaded) are approximate.

CHAPTER 8

"But I Pay More Taxes!"

Even in the early days of his marriage to Helen, Ernie still felt the need to "get out of town" as he had when he was a little boy. The Chenowith area felt familiar from his early days with Grandpa Anderson and "Uncle Pete," riding the hills and hunting "gray diggers" (a very destructive underground squirrel). As a young man, Ernie had spent a lot of time on the hills herding sheep for Bill Ketchum; in his mind he could envision his cattle roaming those hills.

Well established at the harness shop and anticipating a family, Ernie began to watch for property west of town that he could purchase and use for grazing cattle. Many would-be farmers had staked land claims on the hills west of town that would never produce a crop. They built simple structures and when they could not "prove up" on their claim, they left without regret. Consequently, the sheriff advertised property with delinquent taxes and auctioned off such parcels on the courthouse steps. Few people sought pasture land in those days, but that's exactly what Ernie wanted! He bought some of the claims for five or six cents an acre, but once said he thought he averaged about $2.00 per acre for his pasture land.

At a sheriff's sale in October, 1924, Ernie acquired four tracts of land west of town. He bought 320 acres for $244.33. While the parcels were not contiguous, they were fairly close together—it was a beginning. Less than six months later, Ernie and his father purchased a 1,932- acre farm with farmhouses on Five Mile and Eight Mile Creek from Lois Gilpin for $30,000. That property would soon become the winter pasture for Ernie's herd of cattle.

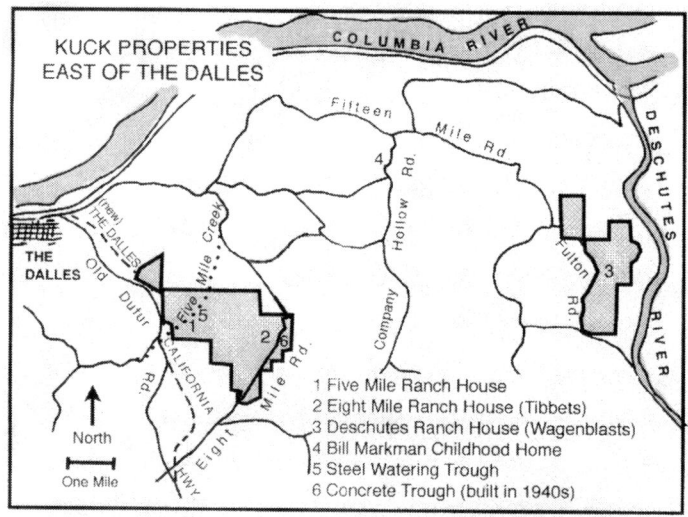

Map created by Irene Hill. Kuck property boundaries are approximate based on information from Bill Markman and legal descriptions interpreted by Ben Beseda, Tenneson Engineering, The Dalles, Oregon.

With that purchase, Ernie owned a wheat ranch, which he then leased because he didn't really want to operate it. In 1935, he approached friend Floyd Tibbets about leasing the Eight Mile place, living in the farm house, and managing the operation. Floyd liked the idea of not "going to work" but "being at work" when he finished his breakfast. He had grown up wanting to be a farmer, and his goal in life was to become a *good* farmer. Financially, he could not buy a wheat ranch, but he understood raising wheat and cattle.

Ernie and Floyd had worked together enough that they understood each other. Floyd had an easygoing temperament and shared Ernie's philosophy of life: If you do a job, do it so it will last; use the quality of material that fits the job to be done; clean up the mess—always be tidy. He knew how to break horses and he had an eye for good conformation. He could fix things, he could remodel buildings, or he could start from scratch and construct "most anything." Kindred spirits, Floyd and Ernie might ride for hours on end without saying a word.

Floyd married Ethel Ulrich, a pretty local school teacher with a pleasant disposition. She rode well, admired Ernie, and loved children. Ernie felt at home with the Tibbets and often bragged about Ethel's good home cooking."

Floyd and Ethel lived in the little white house on Eight Mile Creek and raised a family of lively kids. One of their little girls, Ruth, remembered Ernie. She would position herself behind Ernie's chair when he came to visit. Then she would reach up and rub or pat his head. He brushed her hand away, but pretty soon she'd do it again. Impatiently, Ernie would say, "Stop it!" She stopped, only to wait for another day when he'd sit in a chair where she could reach his head.

Floyd Tibbets operated the ranch for twenty-five years. He reminisced:

> Ernie always left the farming up to me. He knew I'd go ahead with the plowing and the summer fallow. We had 1,400 acres of wheat land. When we brought the cattle down in the fall, we put them out on the stubble field till it snowed; then we'd feed them. We hauled all

the wheat to town—no elevators on the ranch. Ethel drove the wheat truck during harvest and she drove the big caterpillar tractor hauling the hay wagon. I hate to admit it, but women are pretty good drivers. They don't take chances.

When Floyd retired, Earl Wagenblast, oldest son of Henry Kuck's tenants on the breaks of the Deschutes, took over the Eight Mile lease.

Ernie was following in his father's footsteps both in terms of land acquisition and in owner/tenant relationships. In 1892, Henry Kuck had purchased a home in the Laughlin Addition of The Dalles. In 1904, he invested in 640 acres of farm land on the Deschutes and leased it out. Over the next several decades he added adjoining properties, and in 1921, he leased it to Elden Wagenblast's parents, George and May, who managed it until their retirement when Elden assumed the lease. Henry wanted the place kept clean and managed well. Their relationship was based on mutual respect; he never told his tenants what to do. At Christmas, Henry would visit the Wagenblasts and bring a five-pound box of chocolates! In 1934, he gave the kids each a silver certificate.

Elden Wagenblast recalls his mother feeding two crews during harvest, remembering that Henry Kuck would show up with a flat of tomatoes or berries. She'd invite him to come in and eat with the crew. He would always say, "Do I have to wash?" May would shake her head "no," and he would smile and say, "Don't tell my wife."

Ernie kept detailed notes in his "Little Book." Small and unobtrusive, it recorded all his financial dealings. This well-traveled book went everywhere with Ernie. Measuring about

"But I Pay More Taxes!"

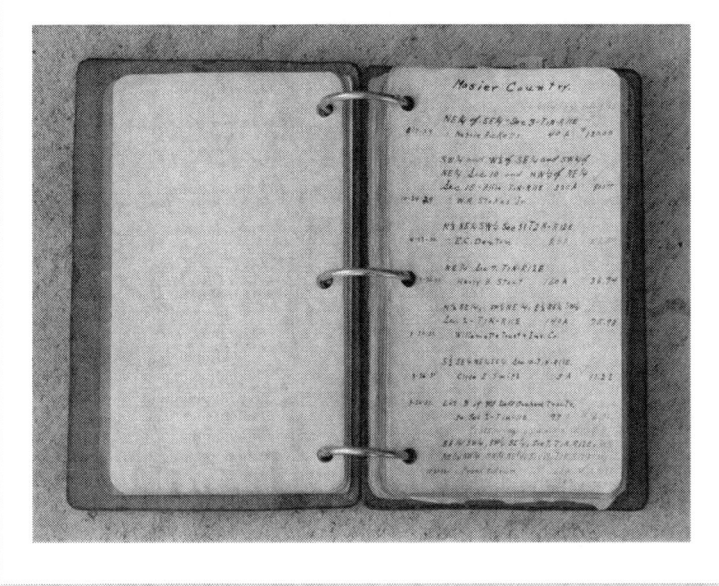

Photos by Jonathan Hill, courtesy of John and Ruth Fulton

five inches by seven inches, it consisted of two leather covers with notepaper between, held together with three metal rings. On those pages, he recorded land that he purchased with the date, legal description, price, and from whom he bought it (see Appendix A). He also listed leases, contracts, cattle sales, ponds, livestock remedies, corral dimensions, family history, health records, and more! All the details of Ernie's life were stored between those leather covers, which he had probably made himself. It was like a loose-leaf notebook; pages could be removed and stowed away for future reference and new pages added for ongoing data.

Ernie, like ol' man Ketchum, acquired neighboring land whenever he could. At some point, the two men agreed to have a certain tree mark the line where neither would buy from the other side. That worked for a while until one day ol' man Ketchum learned that Ernie had bought a tract on the Ketchum side of the tree! Words ensued. Ernie's lame excuse was, "I knew you didn't have money enough to buy it at that time."

The Kuck and Ketchum ranches had adjoining property. Once when Ernie built a fence, Lucile Ketchum thought he was "pushing" their line. Her husband, Bill, and Ernie didn't discuss it; however, when Ernie harvested timber, he had the loggers stop cutting before they reached the fence. Lucile was correct, Ernie had just "borrowed" the use of a sizable tract, but when harvesting the timber, he recognized the legal boundary.

Over the years, Ernie steadily enlarged his holdings, adding parcel to parcel. In 1938, he purchased the Phirman place, which lay south of Doyle Grade on the hilltop with grand views of Mt. Hood and Mt. Adams. Ernie, with Floyd Tibbets help, constructed a cabin there using repurposed lumber from abandoned buildings on his other properties.

"But I Pay More Taxes!"

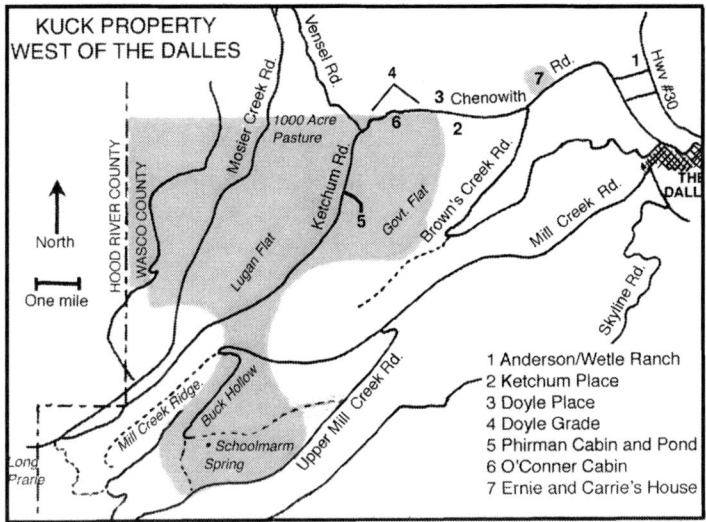

Map created by Irene Hill. Kuck property boundaries are approximate based on information from Ernie's "Little Book," courtesy of John and Ruth Fulton.

Floyd had secured the well-seasoned boards to his horse-drawn wagon and cautiously driven up the narrow, curvy roads to the building site. The finished cabin, nestled among scattered scrub oaks and a few tall pines, provided a base for Ernie and his ranch hands when working cattle.

Through the scattered trees, the peaceful view from the front of the cabin included a slope to the edge of a sizable pond—the Phirman Pond. The board-and-batten outbuildings nearby included a barn to shelter horses and a shed to store hay and grain. A little nearer to the cabin was an outhouse tucked into a clump of shrubbery. Behind the cabin was a spring and cistern etched with Ernie's "Double Lazy A." A little further from the cabin stood the post and pole corrals and fences typical of Ernie's operation.

Fences were a significant investment. Ernie recorded cost and the miles of fence built by different people. In his "Little Book," he noted: "Outside Fence 19-15/16 mile surveyed distance—up and down hills, 2 or 3 miles more," and that was only the perimeter. In another more detailed note he recorded:

May 20 - 1938

Floyd Tibbets, Ralph Doyle, Lewis Robertson, Chad Ulrich

Built fence on Lubin flat and Harper Canyon 1 1/2 mile. = 1 man 44 da. @ $2.50 Da.= $73.34 per mile.

The fences survived the winter differently each year depending on the snow and the way it drifted. Helen Nagle told of one winter when three-fourths of everybody's fences lay flattened on the ground. The weight of the snow had caused the posts to sink down. Sometimes the frozen snow and ice on the wires caused them to break. Repairing fencing by splicing wire and resetting posts sometimes took more than a month. Ernie hired Blaine Miller to build fence on his property—miles and miles of fence. Blaine and his son, Ronal, also built "drift fences" to slow down the blowing snow that might take out regular fences.

One of Ernie's later acquisitions (1949) was the O'Connor place, about seven miles out Chenowith Road. Ernie built corrals and loading chutes for his cattle, but this place also offered a perfect home site to relocate a unique log cabin from another parcel Ernie owned south of Mosier. Ernie had studied the structure, the way the logs fit together, and concluded that Scandinavians had originally built it.

He consulted with Floyd Tibbets about moving the building, which would need to be disassembled, each piece carefully marked, and then reassembled at the new location.

Floyd had a rare ability to know what he could do and what he could not do. He approached the project with organizational skills and quiet confidence. He told Ernie it could be done, and he did it. To this day, paint slashes across some of the logs still demonstrate the code they used so that each log could be replaced in the right location in exactly the right position.

Ernie had electricity installed in his newly placed cabin. The second level boasted a bedroom and bathroom with indoor plumbing! The first level contained the living room/kitchen with a huge stone fireplace anchoring the wall opposite the entry door. The stones on the fireplace surround fit together in such a way that the grout marked out Ernie's "Double Lazy A" brand.

Ernie bought more cattle, and his operation gained momentum. As he continued to acquire more land on both sides of The Dalles, people smiled as they said, "Ernie doesn't want all of Wasco County; he just wants the field next to his." For years he was the largest landowner in Wasco County, with 23,000 acres of pasture and timber. The Hinton & Ward sheep ranch in South County eventually owned more acres, it is true, but with a little twinkle in his eye, Ernie always let it be known, "But I pay more taxes!"

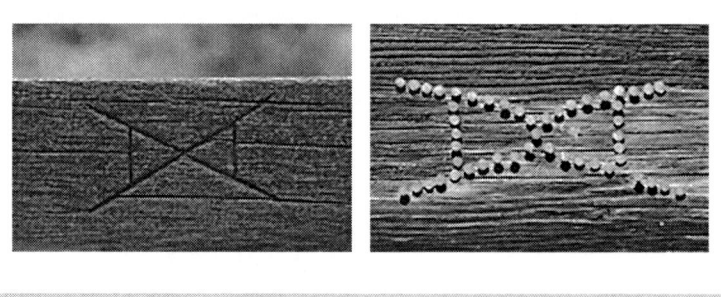

Ernie's "Double Lazy A" branding iron and the "Double Lazy A" etched on a gate and nailed on a building.

Photo of branding iron by Irene Hill, courtesy of Zelta Wasson; other two photos by Jonathan Hill, courtesy of Bill Markman.

CHAPTER 9

The "Double Lazy A" Cattle Company

Ernie's brand, the "Double Lazy A," depicted a pair of tipped-over letter As with their tops touching, creating a flattened cross with the bars of the A in a vertical position. With the initials E.A.K., why would Ernie choose double As? No one seems to know. There are plenty of double As to speculate about: His maternal grandfather was Alexander Anderson; the Anderson brothers, Alexander and George, purchased property in the Chenowith area; and Alexander had two Anderson daughters—Minnie and Nettie (Ernie's mother and aunt). Ernie must have chosen it prior to enlisting in World War I, because the 1918 Oregon Registry of Brands identifies the "Double Lazy A" as belonging to Ernie Kuck. He used this to brand cattle and also to mark some of his gates and buildings.

Ernie continued to acquire land throughout most of his life, and he took to calling each parcel by the name of its original owner. He used land he purchased west of The Dalles for summer forage; he used his ranch to the east for winter pasture. During the 1930s, the central states in America suffered a drought that paralyzed farm operations. With no pasture and no water to be had back there, stock sold cheap. Ernie learned of large numbers of cattle being sold on consignment and he ordered some. When they arrived, they were a sorry-looking lot—a thin, motley assortment of breeds, including longhorns.

Ernie cared for them, brought them back to good health, and put them in with his Herefords. As they reproduced, he weeded out the characteristics he did not want. Eventually, he had a good-sized herd of cattle. He observed that the longhorns produced smaller calves at birth that developed into normal, full-sized animals, so he kept the longhorns with his Hereford cows even though the bulls were mean and would often vie for position in the herd.

In 1933, Ernie applied for a reserve permit and was approved to run twenty-five head of cattle on federal lands managed by the U.S. Forest Service. Eventually, 100 head of his cattle would graze on Forest Service lands.

Forest Service guidelines changed over the years. Friends Joe and Pat Miller said that when they took over their father's operation, they had to prove that they owned enough pasture to handle the stock without using the government land. They puzzled over that requirement for a long time, and finally decided that the government was protecting its resources in case there was a drought and the wild animals needed the grass to eat. They were allowed a given number of "units" (a cow and a calf) for a designated area and they had to be sure to leave 65% of the food for the wild animals. Ernie saw these changing regulations and preferred to keep his distance from government agencies.

All too soon, the endless government rules impacted Ernie and the "Double Lazy A." Reserve permits always specified the allotment (location) being used and the number of animals that could graze in the forest. The Forest Service encouraged

The "Double Lazy A" Cattle Company

fencing to keep cattle within their allotted bounds. During the 1960s, the city of The Dalles, concerned for its water source from the Mill Creek Watershed, required fences to protect the water from livestock contamination. So the Forest Service asked Ernie to fence the land he leased for his cattle.

Occasionally the government built fences, but more often it would provide the metal posts and the barbed wire, while the farmer did the work. It didn't take Ernie long to decide that any fence he built would be on *his* land.

By 1960, Ernie had plenty of summer grazing space for his cattle. He didn't use his reserve permit at all for the ensuing two years. He could have transferred his permit to another rancher, but then he would have had to communicate with the Forest Service. He had not only lost confidence in them, he just plain didn't want to deal with them. He let his permit expire so the Forest Service could re-issue it without Ernie being involved in the transaction at all. The Forest Service, with its requirement to build fences, moved out of Ernie's business altogether.

In the notes about cattle in his "Little Book," Ernie wrote: "1966: All cattle kept inside New Fence"—on *his* land!

Once Ernie hired a complete stranger to plant some posts and string wire around a rocky, steep pasture. Helen Nagle and her stepfather, Ralph Doyle, rode up to see the finished job. Helen quickly noticed how even the posts were–all exactly the same height above the ground. This was remarkable because of all the rocks in the ground. She had dug post holes herself and knew the frustrations of digging them deep enough in rocky soil.

The stranger's posts appeared to be so even! She mentioned it to her dad. He was noncommittal, saying, "Well . . . we'll see." They rode on and he began to veer off away from the fence. She wondered where he was going until he stopped by a pile of post remnants. The fence builder had dug down till he came to a rock, planted the post, firmed up the dirt, and then cut off the post to the correct height. Not only did the job have to be done over, but Ernie now had lots of fence posts too short to use. Ernie confronted the worker and, needless to say, he never worked for Ernie again. Ever!

Ernie constructed his corrals using long poles; he didn't buy lumber. He cut and peeled red fir poles from his property on Chenowith Creek. Somehow, he hauled those long poles on his pickup truck through town to the corrals at Eight Mile and Five Mile without getting a ticket for a load overhang.

Mannie Wasson recollected:

> I built fences for Ernie for a while using pitch posts. That is really the only time I worked for him, but I helped Floyd at Eight Mile Creek quite a bit. A dead pine tree had to be on the ground for some time before the outside layers rotted and fell off the core. Then the pitch developed and hardened. That core never rotted. When the trees were down long enough to be "pitch posts," we'd knock all that rotten wood off and then Floyd would set 'em on fire and he'd burn off all the rest of the loose wood. The pitch wouldn't burn.
>
> Ernie or Floyd would tell us where the pitch logs were that they had burnt. We cut them so they would stand about 5'6" out of the ground when they were set. When we got a length sawn, we just lay it down on the ground and split it with a sledge hammer and wedges into triangular-shaped posts. Out of one big tree we could make quite a lot of posts. I got 10 cents a post and $80 a mile for the installed fence.

The "Double Lazy A" Cattle Company

Ernie wanted things to fit, to be well-constructed, and to last. He also valued convenience. He built all the gates to his corrals and loading chutes in his basement. They were precisely constructed so that each was interchangeable with any other gate, easily slipping over the pivots mounted in the pitch log gate posts. If a rampant steer compromised a gate, the wranglers could easily "borrow" one from a neighboring corral and continue their work.

Ernie built two corral-loading chutes, one at the O'Connor property and one at the Phirman property. They were different from regular gates. At Phirman's old place he designed a chute with traps and funnels so that when one gate was opened, it swung around on a shared post to close another. Sandy Macnab, the county extension agent from 1983 to 2000, recalled:

> Ernie built many corrals but used the same design and building pattern and had some ingenious designs. All the gates were the same size so they were interchangeable, if needed. Pens would hold approximately one truck load of cattle, and he had them built in areas where he could fill them up and then unload them in as stress-free an environment as I have ever seen. Even the loading chutes were eight feet wide so one cow with second thoughts couldn't clog up the system and stop all the others from moving. He had a series of cables and pullies that allowed him to open or close any gate in that particular system, which let him load whole truckloads of stock by himself. Amazing thinker, but awfully quiet.

Unfortunately, the Phirman corrals were destroyed in a lightning fire that engulfed the area during the 1990s.

Bob Sallee recalled:

You know, they used to gather cattle in the mountains in the fall, my granddad and dad, Floyd Tibbets, and Ernie. There was a bunch of them up at Long Prairie. Anyway, it could be miserable weather, cold and rainy. They had to get the cattle out by the first of November. They came in from a day riding up there and my dad says, "You know, I'd give twenty dollars for a jug."

Floyd sez, "I'll go half with you on it."

Kuck's ears perked up, out the door he went, scrounged around in his truck for a while, and came back with a brand new jug. And collected his twenty dollars!

Ernie always had hot chocolate and oatmeal cookies in the glove compartment. He never drank coffee. He never drank liquor. Know what that man ate for breakfast every morning? Oatmeal and soft boiled eggs on toast. And hot chocolate!

Another time Ernie was with a group of riders camping out at Long Prairie. Evening came and dinner was ready, but there was no sign of Ernie! They knew he was riding a young (green) horse. Since Ernie was never late, two young men, Ralph Doyle and Lewis Sallee, saddled up to ride out and find him.

About that time, he showed up, leading his horse with a small bear tied to the saddle. He told his friends that he was on time on the trail when he looked up and saw a small bear in a tree. He got out his little single shot .22 pistol and with many shots, killed the bear. He finally got him down out of the tree, tied him onto the colt, and led the horse back to Long Prairie. They all quickly hung the bear in the woodshed and headed to dinner, his friends marveling that he could tie a bear onto his green horse.

Floyd Tibbets told of another memorable day one fall. With a crisp autumn bite in the air, the cattle had sensed winter approaching and worked their way out of the mountains. Ernie prepared to move them east to the Eight Mile ranch. Floyd remembers:

> One fall just Ernie and I was at the Phirman cabin and it was time to go home with the cattle and it looked stormy.
>
> Ernie sez, "We'd better drive those cattle down to the Doyle ranch today and take an early start there in the morning." We got them all gathered up and we got them out to the main road and a bad blizzard hit. The cows hid in the brush and they wouldn't come out. Ernie said, "We'd better head back to the cabin." So we did, and we stayed all night and that storm was really bad and then it froze.
>
> We got the cattle kicked out of the brush in the morning, on the road and over to the top of Doyle Grade, about two miles long and it was iced over, and those cattle wouldn't walk except way over on the outside where there was a little bit of bare gravel. We had cattle down at the airport and the last ones were still on the mountain, cuz they was single file. Just the two of us. After we got down, people came with their horses and helped us. Didn't lose any. Got home with all of them.

One of Ernie's many eight-sided concrete watering troughs. He built this one in 1936.

Photo by Sandy Macnab, Oregon State University Extension Agent

CHAPTER 10

Springs and Ponds

Cattle need more than just grass and feed to survive; they need water. Ernie's land contained numerous springs bubbling out of the hillsides. As soon as he purchased cattle in 1929, he began to develop ponds and springs on his properties. He cleaned them up and protected the delicate spring sites by building an eight-sided concrete watering trough a little distance away. He would post a small sign designating the name of the pond and used the numbers from an old license plate to note the year it was established. Lastly, he duly noted it in his little leather-backed book.

If a pasture lacked a water source, Ernie and his friend, Art Appling, a hydraulic engineer, would analyze the lay of the land and divert run-off to collect in a concrete watering trough, also named and dated. Sometimes Ernie pumped water to pasture ridges by laying a pipe from Mosier Creek and utilizing a ram pump that operated on the flow of the water and automatically pushed water ahead. A check valve held it in place till more water filled the pipe. Ernie often built watering troughs or sometimes even ponds near the top of ridges. Ernie smiled contentedly as cattle, horses, deer, birds, and all manner of wildlife benefited from his investment.

Ernie developed precise plans to construct his concrete holding ponds. He made easy-to-assemble forms for his eight-sided design and meticulously recorded details of dimensions, materials, and process until he had an exact plan of action. Then he or Floyd Tibbets could load his forms, concrete, hog wire, gravel, reinforcing rods, and pipe onto a string of pack horses and build a holding pond in any remote location—nothing forgotten, nothing extra. Of course, he saved the forms to use again.

Ernie kept detailed notes about his water sources in his little book. He listed springs, cement troughs, and ponds, each with a location, the year it had been acquired or developed, who had helped with the work, and sometimes even the hours of labor and cost of materials.

By 1972, Ernie had developed forty-two ponds. During the 1980s, the Oregon State University College of Agricultural Sciences presented Ernie with the Diamond Pioneer Award. This was to honor those who were seventy-four years old or older and had contributed to the development of Oregon agriculture or natural resources in a significant way. Sandy Macnab, the County Extension Agent during that time, submitted Ernie's name as a candidate for the award. Sandy wrote: "I seem to recall that we emphasized the conservation nature Ernie demonstrated by building so many concrete and earthen dams to collect and store water to be used to water livestock and wildlife; and that enabled him to move cattle from one pasture to another without stressing the stock."

When he developed a water source near a property line, Ernie shared the water with his neighbor. He knew that a farmer could lose his whole operation if he lost a water source. When neighbors expressed their gratitude, Ernie said, "Now don't tell anyone!"

Springs and Ponds

Sometimes the Wasco County Road Department contacted Ernie regarding water diversion, not for stock ponds but for preservation of the county roads. The supervisor, Clayton McCall, remembers that Ernie was always fair. He was willing to negotiate rights-of-way to widen a road or reduce the sharpness of a curve. Sometimes Ernie traded a patch of land and asked for an "in kind" trade, such as grading a road into a stock pond. Clayton said there was not much conversation; most of what he heard from Ernie was "yes" and "no"!

Ernie had no interest in operating heavy equipment, bulldozing, or the mechanical devices that most farmers used. However, he loved to watch heavy equipment at work—sometimes to the annoyance of the friends who were helping him—until they realized that he was completely intrigued by the machines that accomplished so much so quickly in the hands of a skilled operator.

Joe Miller told about using big equipment for Ernie:

> I'd be working and Ernie'd be over there laying on his back propped up on a rock with his hat pulled over his head, watching me, and that got on my ding-dong. I didn't like it! He did the same thing down here after the '64 flood. He had me take my Cat down to help him out. The flood had just about undermined his barn. So there he was, up in the hayloft lookin' right straight down at me, every pass I'd go by the barn. Finally I got off the tractor and went up there and said, "Am I doin' this damn thing right, Ernie?"
>
> "Doin' fine, doin' fine," said Ernie, "but I just love to watch that machine push."

Pat Miller recalled, "Ernie sat in the pickup with me one day up at the Phirman place, and said he liked to watch Joe work with his Cat."

Another time, Joe Miller postponed a job he needed to get done so he could help his friend Ernie, who had a real emergency. A big D8 Caterpillar (about thirty ton) was mired in one of Ernie's ponds. The longer the owner worked to get it out, the more entrenched it got. So Ernie called Joe. With the help of Joe's smaller tractor, a D4 (about seven and one-half ton), they got the big Cat out of the mud in about four hours. Ernie watched the whole operation from a spot up the hill.

Ernie asked Joe how much he owed him for pulling out the big Caterpillar. Joe said his fee was $50 an hour and he guessed he had worked about four hours. Ernie gave him $300. When Joe protested, Ernie quieted him by saying firmly, "If it weren't for you, I'd still be in that mess." Ernie was aware of the cost of things, but he also appreciated the value he received from a job well done.

When the State Highway Department was working on the new highway to Dufur, Oregon, they used heavy equipment to make a cut through the hillside that would let them widen the paved road. Ernie saw the equipment and pulled off the road to watch the big rigs. He took in the whole operation. Preparing to leave, he pulled over to speak to another man watching the work, who happened to be the surveyor on the job. Ernie told the "spectator" that the operators of those machines were surely doing a good job, "But that guy sitting in that little green car over there hasn't done a damn thing." The surveyor didn't tell him that the man in the little green car was the project engineer, and it was his duty to observe as they worked. But he lost no time in telling the project engineer, Vernon Shull, about Ernie's observations.

Springs and Ponds

In another one of Joe Miller's amusing anecdotes, he remembered a day in 1949:

> Ernie come out here one Sunday, and my dad had a bandana around his neck because he had tonsillitis. Ernie also had a bandana around his neck because of tonsillitis. He asked my dad, he sez, "Jess, let's go in and have our tonsils out."
>
> Dad sez, "Oh, I'm about over mine."
>
> "No you aren't!' sez Ernie. "You are always bothered by your tonsils and so am I."
>
> Ernie then asked my mother, "Marie, if we go into the hospital and have our tonsils out, could I come out and stay two weeks?'
>
> Mom sez, "You bet!" So they went in and had their tonsils out. How many days were they in the hospital, five days, six days? When the hospital released them, Ernie got dressed real fast and he disappeared. Dad and Mom went down to pay for Dad's bill, and the billing clerk said that Mr. Kuck had already taken care of it. Ernie stayed out here two weeks. He wanted to recuperate here and eat here.

"Ernie could be hard to deal with for some people," said Mannie Wasson:

> My friend Chuck said he couldn't communicate with Ernie at all, and he wanted me to go talk to him about a lease. Chuck was used to the "warming up and all the little exchanges," and Ernie didn't need or understand small talk. Talking about money, like how much for a cow and a calf, Ernie just sat there when I

was dealing with him and I just waited. It might seem like a long time, but when he finally answered, that was the way it was. He was very sharp.

At one time, fellow cattlemen Chuck Petroff and Mannie Wasson each proposed a lease agreement to Ernie. He listened, then said he would get back to them. Several weeks later, he accepted their terms. Later, they learned that he had first talked to other possible renters but he couldn't get a better offer.

CHAPTER 11

The Great Cattle Drive

Ernie's friend Dee Thompson once asked him, "Why don't you write down how you drove your cattle down through The Dalles?"

He said, 'Nobody would be interested.'

Dee told him, "Yes, they would be. I know people would be interested."

There are many stories about Ernie's cattle drives between 1929 and 1949. The following chapter depicts a typical cattle drive and some of the actual events that occurred over the years as the cattle were moved across town.

Along with the arrival of spring came the long-awaited cattle drive that moved Ernie's herd through town to summer pasture "out Chenowith." In the early days, they tried to drive the cows with their calves all the way through town, but if a calf wandered away from its mother, the mother always turned back to find her baby, creating chaos. So Ernie separated the calves ahead of time and trucked them out to the Phirman place, where he gave each one a shot and branded it with the "Double Lazy A." The steers were also "cut" (castrated) at that time.

The animals who had been on the cattle drive before knew the route, and the first-timers followed along. Horsemen always

Cattle approaching the intersection where East Ninth and Tenth Streets conjoin in The Dalles. On the far right is Jake Grossmiller riding "Chubby."

Photo from author's personal files

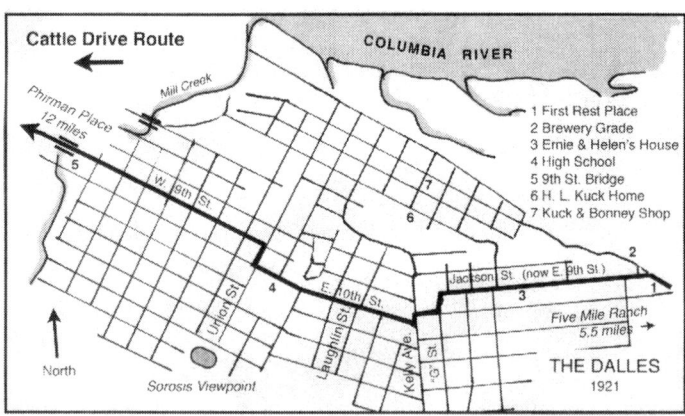

Map created by Irene Hill based on a map of The Dalles, 1921, by P. W. Marx, city engineer, archived at the Columbia Gorge Discovery Center, The Dalles, Oregon.

The Great Cattle Drive

stood ready at the intersections to keep the herd together and out of the carefully-tended front yards of the houses along the route. This activity provided an opportunity for young riders to learn the unique skills involved with herding cows. A few riders would ride ahead and ask people to turn off sprinklers, which might tempt a thirsty cow.

Young people and kids liked being part of the big cattle-driving operation. Three of the Nagle girls, Helen, May, and Florence, would ride all the way from the Doyle ranch on Chenowith to the Five Mile Ranch adjacent to the Eight Mile Ranch where the cattle had been corralled. They then returned, helping to drive the cattle—a round-trip of about twenty-five miles. Florence, who loved to ride bareback, did the whole trip without a saddle—much to her sisters' chagrin. She insisted that "riding bareback you got the feel of the horse, hot and wet."

Ernie would line up some of the regulars ahead of time to be sure there would be enough riders when they started. He knew others would join in as the herd passed neighboring ranches. The cattle drive would take off at daybreak, as soon as riders had finished the hearty cowboy breakfast prepared by Ethel Tibbets.

A couple of men would lead the herd to set the pace. Ernie always said, "A slow walk for a horse is a fast walk for cattle." Their route led them down Auction Yard Hill on the Old Dufur Road, past the Cyphers' farm, and up the hill to a large, bare, flat field above The Dalles where they stopped to rest. That area is just east of the top of Brewery Grade and, at that time, was totally undeveloped. When the whole shebang started up again, they would travel west on Ninth Street until a bluff blocked their way. Then the route turned south on "G" Street for one block, then west again on Tenth Street.

Extra horsemen would wait at the large, unwieldy intersection of Tenth and Kelly to keep the herd on the planned route. Heaven forbid that some of the stock should head north on Kelly and go downtown—or mosey south on Kelly to investigate a few lush flower beds. It probably would have been easier if some of the housewives had not been aggressively protective of their yards.

One year, a homeowner whose house was above the street level came out on the pavement waving her broom and her apron at the cattle. She intimidated one of the young animals and the cow raced north down Kelly Avenue. Ernie commandeered Pat Miller's horse because it was faster than his own mount and raced after the escaping cow. The cow turned on him and knocked Pat's horse down. Ernie returned with the wayward animal, but Pat's beautiful sorrel horse had sustained skinned knees during the encounter. Pat was very upset, and thought she should not ride an injured horse.

Ernie sternly instructed, "Pat, get on that horse and ride it or its knees will get stiff."

Pat got on and rode.

The leaders passed the high school, located between Washington and Union Streets, then turned north on Union for one block to Ninth Street, where they headed west again to cross the Ninth Street bridge over Mill Creek.

Little Jake Grossmiller, on his black Shetland pony, Chubby, rode the sidewalk on the south side of the herd as they entered Ninth Street. All the cattle moved along smoothly until another cattle-hating, protective housewife yelled at little Jake, telling him to get off her sidewalk! She turned her hose on him. The cattle, although usually attracted to water, kept moving. Startled, Jake remembered that he needed to keep

The Great Cattle Drive

those animals out of the front yards, so he rode on, wet from head to toe. Some of the men were seriously annoyed with that housewife and what she had done.

Incidents like this probably happened to other riders along the length of the herd, because they decided that the next year, they should stay on Tenth Street for a few more blocks before they turned to Ninth. However, no one informed the cows, who had been traveling that route for years. Their instincts guided them and, when a horseman tried to stop them from turning north on Union, they kept trying to take the old route. Soon they milled around the intersection becoming totally unmanageable. The crew finally relented and let the cows follow the old route to Ninth Street. The lady with the hose got another chance at Jake.

One year at Seventh Street, Mr. Karamentos had just finished watering his lush, carefully tended vegetable garden. A young heifer went berserk and escaped into his yard. No one knows whether she was running to the newly watered vegetable garden or running away from Pat Miller, who was hard after her. Mr. Karamentos reached to pull the gate shut behind him when the wild cow ran in. He grabbed his hat and waved it at the animal, trying to deflect its path—all to no avail. He and the terrified cow went around the garden a few times, slipping and sliding in the mud until the heifer ran out the gate. Pat directed it back toward the main herd and Dick Shunke bulldogged her on the Ninth Street Bridge.

When things went awry, Ernie would hear about it. In this case, Pat told him immediately. Chuck Uren, a local policeman, told Ernie he might have a lawsuit on his hands. Ernie didn't reply.

A couple of days later, Ernie went into Mr. Karamentos'

shoe repair shop downtown and said, "I understand you had a wild cow in your garden." Mr. Karamentos explained what had happened in vivid detail.

Ernie said, "I am here to pay damages. How much do I owe you?"

Mr. Karamentos said, "No, Mr. Kuck, no. No. Well . . . when you butcher, you could bring me a couple of steaks."

Ernie went to the meat market and bought half a dozen thick, juicy prime steaks for the Karamentos family. Ernie had chosen to put his own price on the mishap, and he paid the damages as he assessed them.

On the first lot east of the Ninth Street Bridge, Dr. Morse owned a new home with a lawn that was well-started, but he refused to turn off his sprinklers. "Let the cows come get a drink," he said. The riders tried to protect that yard, but a few got past them to the water. There were no complaints from the good doctor, who had grown up on a cattle ranch in eastern Oregon.

The riders would try to keep the cattle bunched together, but the herd of a couple hundred head stretched from the high school to the Ninth Street Bridge—a distance of about ten blocks. When they reached Cherry Heights Road, they turned south for a block to turn west again on Chenowith Road. That corner, called Snipes Acres, had few buildings on it in the early days. The drive usually stopped there, but during the last few years of the drive, that corner had been developed. They had to go on to the only open space remaining—a sandy lot south of the Columbia Basin Care Facility (originally the "Poor Farm") for the noon break. The wives of the riders brought lunch by car, so there was always plenty to eat.

Jake and little black Chubby rode with the group west as

far as the Chenowith Grange, where Jake's mother met him and walked back with him to their home on Chenowith Road. The rest of the riders drove the cattle on to Doyle's place (now Sallee's), where there was a big watering trough for the cows, a big coffee pot for the riders, and space to bunk some of them. Then they went on a short distance, where the cattle stayed overnight. The next day was easy—just a few miles farther up the hill before reaching the summer pasture.

According to Ernie, the last cattle drive through town took place in 1949. Ernie had purchased a big green KB-8 International truck to haul his cattle to summer and winter pasture. Civilization had crowded in on the cattle drive route. More people and more housing developments had eliminated the open spaces. Heavier traffic and intolerant housewives abounded. Only the riders were still enthusiastic. No one recorded an opinion from the cows.

The drama and excitement of the old-time cattle drive became a thing of the past, but the wonderful memories lived on in the stories told to grandchildren.

Ernie Kuck

Photo courtesy of Max Post, son of Carrie Kuck

CHAPTER 12

"I Don't Think It's Near That Funny!"

As a kid, Joe Miller rode for Ernie Kuck, who was a good friend of his father. He enjoys telling about basing at the Phirman place to round up cattle. He conceded that he and the other riders always had a good breakfast. Before they would head out for the day, Ernie would get the carton of Hershey bars down from the cupboard and give one to each boy. That was lunch. They rode long days and got in after dark, which they didn't like "worth a darn," but there was always a wonderful, big meal waiting at the end of the long, tiring day.

According to Elden Wagenblast, Ernie "wasn't above playing a trick on you. One time we had a couple of cows and he said it was no use to lead 'em, so we just followed them. I was getting pretty hungry, so I suggested we stop and eat, but he said, 'No, we have to follow those cows.'

"We came to a watering hole and the cows were drinking. Ernie was up ahead, so I could see him clearly. I saw one hand go down behind the saddle, then the other hand came up. I rode up alongside of him and he was eating his peanut butter and jelly sandwich. I said, 'Darn you! You didn't say anything, did you?' He just a-busted out laughing."

An acquaintance, Wayne Huskey, once found one of Ernie's cows that had been shot. Still a schoolboy, he dutifully called to tell Ernie. Ernie said, "Well, son, why don't you just own up to it? You'll feel better!" Ernie's implied accusation startled Wayne. It took an arranged meeting with Ernie for Wayne and his father to convince Ernie that Wayne was being a good neighbor and not a stealthy stalker.

Bob Sallee related the following story:

> Ernie, Floyd, and I took off from the Phirman place in the fall. He was after some cattle back there on the mountain. We rode clear over to where you could look down on Parkdale, and that's a pretty good hike 'cause you gotta cross Mosier Creek. Anyway, we found those cattle tracks in the snow, but pretty soon we lost them. They got down in lower country where there was no snow, so we had to ride all the way back to the Phirman place without the cattle. It was way after dark when we got back and I mean we were freezin'-cold miserable. Ernie sez, "You guys put the horses away and I'll get a fire goin."
>
> Floyd and I took care of the horses. Kuck went into the cabin and got the fire stoked up. It was nice and warm in there. He fixed coffee for Floyd and hot chocolate for himself and me. We sat there telling stories, which was highly unusual for Ernie. He told us about his life just after he got out of the service.
>
> He had an old Model T that wouldn't climb a steep hill because the cars back then didn't have a fuel pump and the gas got to the motor by gravity flow. They simply turned around and backed up the hill and the gas flowed into the carburetor just fine.

"I Don't Think It's Near That Funny!"

Then we got to talking about backpacking. Ernie and a friend of his would backpack over to Badger Lake, go down Gumjuwac Saddle, and down to the lake. He was a small man, but he could carry a full backpack with all the necessities.

In another story, Bob Sallee tells about a time when cowboy Vern Campbell was surprised to get a phone call from Ernie. In his customary fashion, Ernie used few words; he just asked Vern to come down to the shop and talk. When Vern arrived, Ernie told him, "Charlie Bernard has a job for you."

So Vern called on Charlie Bernard, a well-known rancher, who said, "Ralph Doyle and I have a place at Suplee. [Suplee Flats is just past Madras, Oregon, on the way to Prineville, Oregon.] Ralph has been over there working with some horses. He broke a horse for Ernie, and Ernie wants you to ride over to Suplee and bring it back to The Dalles."

Vern agreed, so Charlie continued, "The first night, you'll stay at Maupin, and here is money for the stable, your room, and some to pay for your meals. The second night, you'll stay at a ranch at Willowdale, so it won't cost you. The third night, you'll stay at Madras, and here is money to stable your horse, get a room, and pay for supper and breakfast. The next day you ride over to Suplee and you'll be at the ranch."

Vern took off, did as he had been told, and arrived at Suplee in good time to pick up the horse. To get acquainted with it before he started home, he rode it a little. It was so well broke and had such an easy gait that he rode it all the way to The Dalles, leading his own mount. He arrived in The Dalles, took the horse to the stable, and then checked in with Ernie. Ernie asked how much he owed him. Vern told him the amount. Ernie was unpleasantly surprised at the sum and said, "Well! You might just as well keep the horse, then!"

Vern said, "Fine!" turned around, went out the door, and continued down the street.

When Ernie recovered from his shock at the reply, he realized Vern was not coming back to dicker. He ran out the door in a flash, calling to the vanishing Vern, "Campbell, come back here! Campbell! Campbell! Come back!"

It was a rare thing for Ernie to be talkative. Mannie Wasson described Ernie as quiet. "You know, he said so little . . . I have rode with him all day long and sometimes not say more than a dozen words. He'd answer you if you asked him a question, but to make conversation, you know, he wasn't . . . There had to be a reason for talking."

Mannie and his son, Monte Wasson, sometimes helped at the Phirman place, rounding up cattle. On one occasion the weather turned really cold, so the next day Monte wore a warm cap that covered the back of his neck and included ear muffs. When he walked into the barn to get his horse, Ernie took one look at him and said, "What's on your head?" Monte said it was a cap to keep his ears warm. Ernie said, "You are not riding with me today looking like that." So Monte had to ride with his dad or Floyd. It warmed up, and the next time Monte wore his western hat. Ernie looked at him and said, "That's better. You go with me today!"

Monte Wasson also remembers that, as a teenager, he was rounding up cattle with Ernie during a period of bad weather. The snow and rain caused the cattle to want to stay in the bushes, so Ernie went in after them. When he came out, he had no hat and his glasses were hanging on one ear. Monte couldn't keep from laughing. Ernie scowled at him and said, "I don't think it's *near* that funny!"

CHAPTER 13

Accidental Money

One day, a logger asked, "Ernie, when are you going to log that timber you have up on Mosier Creek?" Ernie denied having timber land—he owned pasture. The logger flashed a knowing little grin and suggested that Ernie go by and look at it sometime.

Ernie went to investigate. He described that visit as the first time he really looked at the trees. He looked at the corners, where years ago he had pulled the barbed wire tightly around a young tree trunk. The wire was now coming out of the middle of a great big tree! He contacted the logger and before long, the timber was being harvested. The amount on the check when they settled up simply amazed the frugal cattleman.

Ernie's "pastures" produced a lot of timber. When he had purchased the land during the 1920s and 1930s, the logging industry had lacked heavy equipment to safely harvest trees on steep slopes. After World War II, however, equipment could handle big trees, no matter how steep the terrain. As the economy strengthened, the demand for timber increased and Ernie began to sell his timber to a number of loggers.

Once Ernie sold the timber off the pasture that goes down into Mosier Creek and Lugan Valley. He explicitly told the company that had the contract to stay back a specified distance from the road. The logging outfit started to cut trees right next to the road. When Ernie saw the felled trees, he warned the loggers to tell their boss that if more trees were cut near the road, it would cost them. Ernie checked again and found more trees cut down along the road. Ernie expected people to honor agreements to the letter and this outfit was showing itself to be untrustworthy, so he cancelled the contract right then and there and demanded reparation.

Elden Wagenblast told the following story, which would be a fit ending for this incident. Elden didn't recognize a man who walked into the sporting goods store. Ernie stood up. The man walked up to him and handed him a check. Ernie looked at it, folded it, and put it into his pocket. The man walked out. No words were exchanged. With a grin, Elden said, "Boy! I wish I knew what that guy had done to Ernie!"

Ernie soon learned which loggers he could trust. Those who failed to honor their word no longer existed in Ernie's world. In Ernie's opinion, they ranked right up there with ever-changing and increasingly burdensome government regulations.

A new rule surfaced from the Forest Service: If you clear-cut a tract, you had to replant it or change the use of the property. While Ernie recognized the Forest Service's role of management, his reaction to someone telling him what he "had" to do with his own property was predictable.

Inevitably, some of his logging contracts required that he replant seedlings. Forester John Buckman saw Ernie in his pickup one day. Ernie rolled down the window and John talked to him about the issue. Ernie listened quietly, but his face turned pink and then red, he pursed his lips, and the forester reports that, "Suddenly, he rolled up the window of his pickup. He just drove off and left me there beating my gums." John concluded the story, saying, "On the whole, the Forest Service got along fine with Ernie."

Later, the Forest Service offered excess inventory of nursery trees to the public at no cost. Never one to turn down a good deal, Ernie picked up his quota of young trees and planted every one. If they were fruit trees, he left the crop for wildlife to enjoy.

Years later, Bob Sallee asked Ernie, "How come you logged this all off?" He replied, "At the time, the state was coming through cruising timber and figuring taxes on ripe timber. They forced me to log it. They literally forced me to log it." Bob said, "He logged all that country up there in the '50s, and I can remember a lot of that timber as the trucks went down Chenowith and then up around Browns Creek and down Cherry Heights. The full loads were too heavy to go across the Chenowith Bridge out there. I watched trucks go by with one log to a truck."

Joe and Pat Miller told a story of a neighbor adjoining one of Ernie's Chenowith properties. When Ernie prepared to cut the timber on his property, he learned that he had environmentalists for neighbors. They had built their barn-like house near the boundary of their property, which also happened to be next to Ernie's timber. The woman and her mother objected strenuously to the prospect of Ernie's woodland being timbered off.

Unmoved, Ernie continued his plans. He arranged with the loggers to keep the access road watered down to protect the lady from dust. Every time she saw him, she told him he shouldn't cut those wonderful big fir trees. She tried to convince him once too often.

She tried to tell him what he could do with his own property (always a red flag to Ernie), and he resented it. He contacted the logger and cancelled the water trucks on site. The west wind steadily blew dust into the woman's house and yard. Ernie later admitted, 'It was a dirty trick to do, but I got tired of listening to her. She told me that I couldn't cut my own trees down!'"

He described his logging income as "making money accidentally," and often said, "I made more money accidentally than I ever did on purpose!"

Joe Miller recalled a time that Ernie came to the home of Joe's parents, Jesse and Marie, for dinner. After the meal, the men moved to the living room and settled into comfortable chairs. Jesse sat in his old rocker.

Ernie pulled out his wallet, took out a check, and reached over to hand it to Jesse. It was a $31,000 timber check. Recalled Joe:

> That was more money than Dad had ever seen!
>
> Dad sez, "That took a lot of timber, didn't it, Ernie?"
>
> Ernie sez, "Oh, a few trees."
>
> Ernie put the check back in his wallet and pulled out another one for $96,000. Dad just looked at it and gave it right back!
>
> Dad said to me, "Just imagine carrying that amount of money around!"

On another occasion, Bob's mother, Helen Sallee, was riding in the pickup with Ernie, taking hay to the animal shelters at his line cabins. They hit a big bump, knocking the glove box door open. A check drifted to the floor. As she picked it up, she noticed it was a timber check for $15,000. She asked Ernie why he hadn't deposited it, and Ernie replied, "That's from the sale of timber off of property that I paid a nickel an acre for."

Ernie once asked another passenger to get something out of the pickup glove box. A check for $75,000 fell out. It was timber money, casually stuffed into the catch-all glove box. The surprised passenger marveled at a check of that size being in the glove box!

Ernie didn't brag or exaggerate; however, a glimpse of a timber check might have been a very subtle and silent way of hinting about the financial success of the "worthless pasture" he owned.

Ernie told friend Bill Markman about other timber checks he had received during the 1950s. Bill remembers the mention of a payment of $450,000. But when sharing pithy words of financial wisdom with Bill, he often repeated, "When you get your calf check, get it into the bank right away! Don't wait till tomorrow! Let it start working for you today." No one ever saw a "cattle check" in Ernie's glove box!

It appeared that Ernie viewed timber checks differently from the money he earned from his cattle business. "Income" had to cover business expenses, and every penny saved looked good on the accounting pages. He had invested sweat equity in his cattle income. On the other hand, he had purchased "worthless" land to use for pasture. When he bought some of the tracts, they already had big trees growing in locations inaccessible to logging at that time. He was buying pasture for his cattle. He didn't anticipate an additional source of income.

Timber money was a surprise bonus. As mentioned, Ernie often said, "I've made more money accidentally than I ever made on purpose."

CHAPTER 14

"Now Don't Tell"

During the 1930s, Ernie's sister-in-law, Hazel Huntington Gronewald (mother of the author of this book), taught school in The Dalles. When she received her paycheck, she went to town to pay bills. Somehow, one month she got to town before the bank opened. Stymied until she had cash, she went to the sporting goods store to see if Ernie could cash her check. He opened the till and shook his head, then reached for his wallet and cashed the check—her total monthly income—out of his own wallet! Flabbergasted, she shook her head repeatedly during the day. "Imagine carrying that much money in a billfold!" she said.

But on at least one occasion that was not the case. Ernie went to lunch with Art Sharp at the old "Hoot Owl Cafe." He and Art were both ranchers and often rode together and helped each other with their operations. Although Art was as tall and muscular as Ernie was short and wiry, they thought alike and were good friends—except at lunch. As Joe Miller tells it:

> They was always gettin' in an argument as to who was going to pay for the meal. They had finished their dinner and Art got up and he said, "I'll get this meal."

Ernie sez, "No! I'll get it."

They argued back and forth and finally Art sez, "Okay, if you are going to be that way." And Ernie didn't have his checkbook and not a dime in his pocket. Art sez, "I told you you was broke!" And Art ended up paying for the dinner.

What to do with all that timber money? Economic conditions had changed. Ernie had already purchased sufficient acreage for his herd. He chose to invest in negotiable certificates of deposit, known as CDs. If interest went up, he could take advantage of it, and he knew what a difference even a quarter of a point of interest would make in the value of an investment. He preferred the stability of tax-free CDs instead of risking the irregularities of the ever-shifting stock market. He kept a record of his CDs in his little leather book and took advantage of any increase in interest rates.

Ernie claimed that his favorite hobby was "making money," which might more accurately have been expressed as "collecting CDs." He knew exactly how many he owned and the interest on each one. If he could get better interest on a different issue, he was able to "roll them over" to his benefit. This seemingly simple technique was validated by the size of the estate he left behind.

Local doctor and history buff Paul Vogt remembers meeting Ernie in the bank parking lot. Ernie had just come out of the bank wearing a big smile instead of his usual dour expression. Dr. Vogt said, "Ernie, you must have shafted someone, 'cause you are smiling."

Ernie said, "I just had a strange thing happen. I rolled over some CDs and the girl got a little excited and I came away with an extra CD." Paul asked how much it was for, and with a twinkle in his eye, Ernie replied, "It was only $500,000. . . I'll let her go through her books for a while, then I'll go back and straighten her out . . . She'll have a heart attack if I don't." Ernie and Paul chuckled quietly together.

Terry Alfson, Ernie's investment broker, described Ernie as a "hands-on" investor. Ernie ultimately accepted Terry's advice, but at first he would back away, be gone two or three months, then come in again. One time he said, "I should have listened to you earlier." Terry told Ernie that he wasn't very good at choosing investments. "Buying government bonds is like dancing with your sister; all it does is generate income." Terry believed that if Ernie invested in growth funds, he could double his money. When interest rates soared, Ernie sometimes earned up to $1,000,000 a year in interest income.

Ernie would visit with Terry if he met him on the street. Terry went on to reminisce: "I earned his respect by standing up to him, telling it like it was. Ernie would 'push,' but he had respect for those who called him on it. Once you earned his trust you were in with him forever." Terry added, "I finally got him to smile."

While some folks perceived Ernie as rich and miserly, Carol Daniels remembers him as a wonderful, caring man and a good friend who would give you the shirt off his back if you needed it. He had no interest in status or position, but just wanted to be seen as a "common man." Carol said he was not stingy, but very charitable.

Over the years, Ernie quietly assisted farmers and friends probably more often than anyone realized. He always admonished them, "Now don't tell anyone." Joe Miller told the following story about Ernie and Joe's father, Jesse Miller:

Mrs. Jensen wanted to sell her place and Sherman Brock wanted to buy it, but he didn't have the cash and couldn't seem to find any. He asked my dad, who assured him that if he had it, he would give it to him, but he didn't have it.

Sherm asked, "Where in the world, Jesse, would a private party loan me money?"

Dad sez, "I don't know. Go see Ernie Kuck."

"Oh," Sherm sez, "That tightwad wouldn't loan me even three cents!"

"Have you ever asked him?"

"No, and I am not going to ask him."

"All Ernie will say is 'yes' or 'no.'"

About a week later, Sherm got the guts to go see Ernie. Ernie sez, "How are you going to pay it back if I loan it to you?"

Sherman wanted to pay Mrs. Jensen cash for her property. "I can pay you so much a month and you name the interest; I don't mind paying interest. You name it."

Ernie sez, "I'll charge you 6 percent interest. When do you have to have the money?"

"Just as soon as I can get it, 'cause I'm scared to death she will sell it to someone else."

"I'll give you a check right now, and you go by and show it to her tonight so she knows you have the money. Then go to town and cash it in the morning and pay her."

"Now Don't Tell"

That is the way Sherman Brock bought that property. But it was about five-—maybe four—years later they began to get really friendly, going on trail rides and camping overnight and everything.

Sherman later told me, "That man Kuck is sure to be paid on time, or before time, every month when I get my check." And Sherm kept his word, too!

Joe Miller told a story about his brother, John. John wanted to buy a used Caterpillar for $1,500 cash. He'd found a good deal and he needed a tractor, but he didn't have the money. He went to visit Ernie one evening. As Joe recalled:

Ernie was reading the paper. John got to talking but didn't come to the point. Finally, Ernie set the paper aside and said, "What's on your mind, John? Spill it out."

"Well," John sez, "I'm needing $1,500. I've got a good deal on a tractor in Wasco."

Ernie sez, "You want $1,500?"

"That's what I need."

"You be here in the morning and I'll have $1,500 for you."

He never said interest or a damn thing. He asked John when he expected to pay it back, and John said, "Right after harvest." And that was that.

If Ernie owed money, it was paid—usually a day early, but always on time. If money was due to him, he was aware of the due date. If someone failed to pay him, Ernie would remind him, maybe once. If it was not paid—for Ernie, that person had disappeared from the earth.

Ernie formed an opinion of people as he observed them. Only a few people ever defaulted on a debt to Ernie. If someone asked for a loan, his first question was, "Why?" Then he wanted to know when and how that person could repay it and if he or she had a dependable income source. He usually charged interest at the going rate, but he never gouged anyone by making them pay unfairly high interest.

Ernie made an exception to this general rule when he dealt with youngsters. He observed a boy's demeanor and sometimes made a deal with him, "man to man." Years later, the lucky boy would realize that he had not signed a contract, that he had not paid any interest, and that Ernie had let him take the treasured "purchase" home on his word that he would pay for it.

Betty Kincheloe Broer started working at the U.S. Bank in The Dalles after high school during the late '30s, when employees figured accrued interest using pencil and paper. She told about a new device that revolutionized the banking industry in her time. Those first calculators provided a fast, accurate way to figure interest—except for Ernie Kuck's account. His records had to be sent to Portland, where big calculators had enough place holders to handle the large balance he had on deposit!

CHAPTER 15

Another New Friend

Although perceived to be unsociable, Ernie talked readily on topics of interest to him, especially local history. He had no patience with superficial conversation. He often visited with new people at the Elks Lodge and, if they had not seen the area south of Mosier, he would take them in his pickup and show them the old homesteads and landmarks, the back roads, the scenic spots, and the "footprints" of abandoned buildings. In springtime, he pointed out enormous clumps of daffodils that grew wild from early gardens left by failed homesteaders. He knew every nook and cranny of Wasco County's varied topography, as well as some of Hood River County, where he also owned property. He loved to share the history of the area.

He usually went "out" (from the Elks club) to eat his lunch; but one day, in 1952, he was visiting with a newly transferred member when the noon whistle blew, signaling lunch time. His companion, Frank Falbo, suggested that they eat downstairs at the Elks so they could continue their conversation. Each enjoyed the time together. The following day, they were playing cards together when the whistle blew and they went to the dining room again as if it were the thing to do. They found plenty to talk about, and Frank was a prime candidate for one of Ernie's "show- and-tell" visits to the hills west of the city.

On that first day, Ernie and Frank headed west of town and enjoyed beautiful views of Mt. Adams and Mt. Hood as they took note of the Phirman place, the Leininger place, Leaning Tree Pond, and other old homesteads west of The Dalles. The two men shared their mutual interest in local history as they drove through Ernie's vast accumulation of land.

Frank would go with Ernie on any of his ranch trips as long as they took the pickup truck. Frank hated horses. Since Ernie constantly kept a check on the soundness of his fences, the condition of his springs and water sources, and any loggers that had contracts to work on his property, Frank and Ernie spent many hours together riding in that pickup.

When asked what they found to talk about in the long hours they shared, Frank thought for a moment, looked off into the distance, and a little grin crept over his face. He almost whispered, "We ran the whole world." He and Ernie had become confidants.

Frank related how Ernie would sometimes leave, saying, "I have to see my lawyer." Ernie might or might not explain why, but Frank never asked. Occasionally, Ernie would confess a donation he had made to some charity, with the customary, "Don't tell anyone." And even though Ernie didn't really talk about it, Frank knew that Ernie made loans to farmers to help them save their farms. Sometimes it would slip out, but Frank kept such confidences to himself, and their friendship strengthened over time.

Frank and Ernie's lunch routine at the Elks endured for years. The waitresses got to know the two men so well that sometimes they just brought their lunch without an order, since the two men ate pretty much the same food every day. On Mondays,

Wednesdays, and Fridays, Ernie paid. On Tuesdays, Thursdays, and Saturdays, Frank paid. They never argued about the bill.

Frank related the following story:

> Ernie liked his hobby, which was making money. One time, someone came into the Elks Club showing off a huge, fancy belt buckle. He asked Ernie how he liked it. Ernie said, "Pretty good. Where did you get it?"
>
> "The bank gave it to me when I bought a $10,000 CD."
>
> Ernie replied, "I don't care about the buckle, but what is the interest?"
>
> I think that is when interest had started to go up, and the man replied, "8.75 percent."
>
> I could see that glitter in Ernie's eyes.
>
> Soon Ernie said, "I'll be back, Frank." About ten minutes later, he came back and he had bought two certificates at that bank. He said, "Now don't tell anyone."
>
> They were both $100,000 CDs. I said, "Where is my belt buckle?" He said, "Good Heavens! I'll go get you two of them."
>
> I said, "I don't want them, they are so big and heavy, they would pull my pants down." Ernie wasn't interested in the belt buckle either . . .

Frank's wife, Velma, enjoyed Ernie's visits to their home and often served warm, homemade bread with jelly. Frequently she sent him home with bread and a fresh jar of her jelly. He appreciated her generosity and always returned the little jar, clean and shiny and full of pennies for her to contribute to a group that saved pennies to benefit children.

Carrie Kuck

Photo courtesy of Max Post, son of Carrie Kuck

CHAPTER 16

Ernie's Second Love

The Fort Dalles Riders formed in 1947, with Ernie as a charter member. He didn't get to all the meetings, but he attended the events that the club sponsored, such as parties and the annual Ft. Dalles Rodeo and parade. These provided an informal social atmosphere where he could watch others and seek out anyone he wanted to talk to. Around 1953 he took special notice of Carrie Smawley, a beautiful divorcee, skilled horsewoman, and one of the first elected officers of the club. He frequently stopped at a restaurant that Carrie managed on the west end of town.

Carrie had a friendly, outgoing personality that people enjoyed. She and Ernie visited. They saw each other at Fort Dalles Riders meetings. They played cards. They rode horseback. They continued to visit and shared memories. Ernie learned about her early life: how she had been orphaned at the age of six and grew up in the homes of various relatives and friends. She learned to "stick up for herself," which she did well. She knew her mind and could maintain her opinion—some folks called it stubbornness.

After graduating from Jefferson High School in Portland, Oregon, she married George Post. They had one son, Max, in

1926 and later divorced. In 1938 Carrie married a member of the Elks, J. K. Smawley, who was a livestock dealer and who, with his brother Lew, operated a secondhand store in Colfax, Washington. J. K. taught Carrie to ride. After their divorce in 1952, she continued to work in restaurants.

Ernie had respect for a person who "stood up to him," and apparently Carrie had that ability. She enjoyed group activities and encouraged Ernie to be more socially active. Ernie was intrigued. Friends began to view them as a couple. Ernie's younger friends, who had not known Helen and Jimmy, often recalled that they had never noticed Ernie smile until he had found Carrie.

Pat Miller recalled how meeting Carrie changed Ernie:

> Up at the Phirman place in the later years, the women would get meals up there, and when I was reaching into the potato sack to get potatoes, I guess my bare hide was showing. Someone came up behind me and ran their thumbnail across my back and I jumped like I'd been shot! I heard someone laughing. I turned and it was Ernie! He'd never done anything like that before! He just seemed to change entirely—all for the better, 'cause he was happy, laughing, kidding, joking!

Carrie and Ernie each had independent temperaments; each had endured the pain of loss and loneliness. Soon, they planned to marry. This news sparked Elden Wagenblast's imagination, and he began to talk to Ernie's friends about a chivaree for the newlyweds. He even told Ernie about his plan. That made it easy for Ernie to avoid the whole thing!

He stopped at the bank one day to get cash for their honeymoon trip to Sun Valley. He had been hauling cattle all day and was wearing his grubby work clothes. He told the new teller that he needed cash and gave her a check for $1,500. She disappeared for a long time. Ernie waited and waited.

Max Kasberger, the bank manager, watched from his office as Ernie paced restlessly. The new teller checked his credentials, as she should have done because she didn't know him; his work clothes, covered with mud and manure did not exactly recommend him. Max finally asked Ernie if he could help him in any way. Ernie explained that the teller had his check and he needed to get home.

"She finished that day and it may have been her last!" laughed Joe Miller, who told the story.

Ernie and Carrie were married in Walla Walla, Washington, on May 13, 1955. They honeymooned in Sun Valley, Idaho, long enough that the plans for a chivaree had evaporated by the time they got home.

Ernie had purchased the home of Judge Ward Webber the week before they married. The 163-acre parcel fronted Chenowith Road. The steep-roofed house sat just off the road, partially concealed by a cluster of trees. They likely spent time at the O'Conner log cabin while they settled into their new home.

Blaine Turner, who lived behind the Webber house, was a dedicated rock hound. Ernie's friends agree that Blaine helped Ernie get started with rock collecting. Stones seemed to call to him. When driving, sometimes Ernie would stop quickly, saying, "Did you see that rock back there? I've got just the place for it." Always prepared, he would contrive to get it into his pickup, using a winch if necessary. In his mind, he knew exactly where it would fit in one of his masonry projects.

One long time project was the construction of a wall at the Webber place. It was high enough to provide unlimited seating around the edge of the concrete patio. To break the monotony of the straight wall, here and there Ernie placed a flat stone to sit on. He positioned stone arm rests on either side. He found all those stones in Wasco County. Ernie really enjoyed constructing that stone wall and a wishing well; however, Carrie did not appreciate all that "junk" on her patio.

Carrie used her culinary skills from her restaurant days to feed Ernie's crews. She'd go up to the Phirman cabin and prepare a meal suited to the hearty appetites that showed up for lunch. After the men went back to work, she'd bake a pie and leave it on the table; sometimes when a couple of young wranglers arrived first, they cleaned it up before the others returned!

Occasionally, Ernie would lead a group—the Fort Dalles Riders or a local 4-H club—up Chenowith Road to the Phirman place for an overnight campout. He developed a number of trails on his property that he named, maintained, and designated accordingly. Tin Can Trail, Pop Can Trail, Buck Horn Trail, and Milk Can Trail were each identified with the appropriate items to mark the path. Milk Can Trail actually led to Milk Can Pond. When enjoying the trails, the young folks especially liked stripping off their horse's saddles and riding their swimming horses in the Phirman pond. Ernie frowned on that, but Carrie advocated on behalf of the kids and they had a wonderful time.

Unfortunately, during one extremely cold winter, the water pipes leading to their house on Chenowith froze. Ernie and Carrie simply endured the inconvenience. One of the neighbors commented, "If the stock was without water, the pipe would have been fixed immediately and— heaven knows—Ernie had the money to have it done!"

In 1979, unwilling to spend another winter like that, Carrie decided she should move into a comfortable mobile home in town. Ernie bought what she wanted and watched as she removed the pieces of living room furniture from the Chenowith house that she wanted to use in her new residence. This left Ernie with some bare spots, so he just brought in the lawn furniture. As his friends told about the furniture, they grinned a little, wagged their heads, and admitted that they thought it kind of humorous.

Ernie's friends smile when they tell of ensuing winters, when heavy snow and lots of ice made driving difficult. Ernie would come in from Chenowith, shop for Carrie, deliver groceries and supplies to her home in town, and then drive back to the Webber house. Carrie probably felt less isolated in winter weather, when she had close neighbors.

Ernie would not—or maybe he could not—leave the home they called the Webber place. He continued to live there. He would see Carrie, sometimes eat dinner with her and visit, but he returned "home" to sleep. When he suffered a chainsaw accident involving one of his knees, he did stay at Carrie's until he could look after himself. At that time, Elden Wagenblast quietly assumed responsibility for keeping a rick of stove-ready wood on the porch at Ernie's house.

Bob Sallee remembers that Mannie Wasson stopped by Carrie's to pay Ernie the rent for his pasture during the time when Ernie was laid up. Ernie accepted the payment and told Carrie that he had to go to town to get that money into the bank. Carrie demurred because she had not planned on going to town that day. Ernie's business sense told him to get that money deposited, so he replied, "Mannie will take me." His maxim to deposit the money "now"—not tomorrow—had asserted itself. And it wasn't a timber check!

Although they lived separately, Ernie and Carrie remained married and devoted to each other. Socially, they were a couple and attended parties and celebrations together. They always visited the Tibbets family at Christmas, sometimes bringing mementos from Ernie's youth as a gift for the children. One year, Carrie divided Ernie's marbles between two of the boys with a little note about how Ernie had played with them. She introduced one boy to collecting souvenir spoons, and Ernie offered them some of his duplicate stamps. These gestures provide plenty of evidence of cooperation between Ernie and Carrie—and mutual appreciation of these valued long-term tenants.

Many people did not recognize Ernie's compassionate side. After he and Carrie married, Ernie often visited Joe Miller's sick mother for an hour at a time. Ernie once told Pat, Joe's wife, "When I ask other people about Marie they say 'She is OK,' but I know when I come to you, I'll get the truth."

Pat added, "Ernie cared. He really cared."

Over the years, the Ketchums, who owned sheep, always welcomed Ernie when he stopped to visit. When "ol' man Ketchum" retired, he often helped his son by herding the flock when it moved to unfenced pasture. Ernie would locate the flock, visit with Bill, and make sure the "ol' man" had enough supplies. This is an example of the respect Ernie felt for his mentor and fellow farmer.

Ernie would sometimes visit young Bill Ketchum and his wife, Lucile, at their home. On occasion, he would leave and then return shortly to tell them that he had seen one of their cows loose on the road. Shaking her head in remembering the incident, Lucile observed, "Not many people would do that, and it is probably the last thing I would ever expect Ernie Kuck to do! He was a good neighbor."

Ernie often enlisted fellow Elk member Frank Falbo to drive him into Portland to visit a sick or ailing Elk member. He seemed to always find time to care for his friends.

When Carrie was diagnosed with cancer, Ernie enlisted the best help he could get for her, and supported her as she fought the disease. She thought she had beaten the "Big C," but when another tumor developed and surgeries and treatments did not stop the metastatic spread of the cancer, she endured it for the rest of her life. She died on April 18, 1993, at the age of eighty-seven, about one year after Ernie's demise.

CHAPTER 17

Five-Star Photographer

A few years after their marriage, Carrie was really stumped to find a gift for Ernie. What can you purchase for someone who can buy anything he wants? You seek something that he would not logically ever think of wanting—but what?

She went to Mel-O's Camera Shop to see what they would suggest. Wilma Roberts, assistant to shop owner Mel Olmstead, helped Carrie select a camera that Ernie might enjoy: a simple-to-operate one that took good pictures. Greatly relieved, Carrie bought the camera. Wilma forgot about the incident until, about a year later, Ernie walked into the store with the camera in his hand.

"Wilma, have you got a better camera than this one?" Ernie asked.

"Yes, Ernie, I have quite a few."

"What is the best one you've got?"

"Oh . . . it is that one . . . up there on the shelf."

"How much is it?"

"It is $595." In those days, that amount of money would buy half a house.

"I'll take it," said Ernie. "You put a roll of film in it and show me how to work it."

"OK, Ernie. I'll do that."

"When I bring this in for processing," he said, "I want you to look at every picture."

Wilma and Ernie got into a regular routine. She explained, "He would buy the film, I would load the camera, and he would take it out and use the film up, and then he would bring it back [to be developed].

"He would ask, 'What could I have done to make this one better? Why does that look like that? What is wrong with this one?' And we would go through all those photographs every time.

"Well, eventually he had quite a little file of the ones Mel Olmstead and I considered the best ones, and Ernie said, 'Now I want to do the same thing you do. I want to send my pictures into that society that you send yours to.'

"I answered, 'Well . . . you have to join the Society, and it is pretty expensive.'

"He answered, 'Oh that's all right.'

"And I thought . . . well, my golly. He probably never, ever saw a slide show or anything, and here he was going to compete with people who scared *me* to death, and I had been around taking pictures for a long time."

Ernie joined "that society," the Photographic Society of America (PSA), in September 1958. Wilma said:

> I showed him how to make out the blanks and how to clean his slides, put them between glass, and tape them. He bought the very best quality mounts—all metal things that I never thought I could afford. Carrie told me later he would spend hours and hours on those things—getting just the right-shaped mount. If the image had too much sky, he would blank that

part out with a mask so the finished slide would look its best on the screen. He hardly ever finished up with a picture that was a full frame. He kept at it, sending them away. Every time the 'report card' evaluation of the pictures came back, he would come in as fast as he could to the store. Mel and I—and maybe Ray McGuire from the *Chronicle*—would discuss our scores. It was a real fun activity for all of us, and we all enjoyed it very much.

He had to learn. It is not something you can just do automatically—like, if you wanted to be an Olympic swimmer, you couldn't just jump into the pool and start right there. You can't teach anybody everything there is to know so they can go out and take a perfect picture the first time. They just have to get burned by making their own mistakes so they can remember what they did. You can get a very staid composition by reading the books on art, but there is a lot in photography that doesn't exactly fit the rules. You run into a lot of challenges that you have to make your own decision about. And a lot of people just don't have that ability.

Ernie would go out and sit all day, waiting for the best light. Sometimes he would return the next day to take advantage of the light on a scene that he wanted to record. He got wonderful pictures.

Sometimes Ernie watched rodeos with camera in hand, anticipating the action shots. At other times, he arranged pictures. While at the Phirman place with friends, Ernie once related, "I caught a rattlesnake down on Mosier Creek, brought him up here, put him on a big stump, and took pictures of him." When asked how he got the snake up to the stump. Ernie said,

Five-Star Photographer

"Coffee can . . . I just caught him with a forked stick, put him in a coffee can and put the lid on, brought him up here, and let him out on the stump." All for the sake of a photo opportunity!

"Of course, Ernie joined the local Camera Club and attended faithfully," observed Wilma. "He always sat in the back row, the last one on the end, and he never said a word. You could never get him to comment. You could never get him to judge. He just sat there and enjoyed."

Said Wilma:

> Time went on and he kept sending his slides away to the society until, within an unheard-of short time, he got his five-star award, which was as high as you could possibly go in that prestigious photographic society.
>
> To give an idea of the competition, one time I went to Forest Grove and judged 2,250 slides in one afternoon. That's what he was competing against. Lots of times the judging would take two days. The slides were graded on a curve. The ones at the top of the grading curve won the gold and silver medals and ribbons, and then there were honorable mentions at the lower level.

Ernie worked diligently and submitted pictures faithfully. The January 1961 *PSA Journal* announced that he had received his One-Star Rating with thirty acceptances and at least six different images. To attain the Five-Star Rating required 640 acceptances with 128 different images. Ernie kept at it!

Wilma added:

> It cost as much to be a Five-Star exhibitor in the Photographic Society of America as it did to own a

Cadillac. I finally dropped out of the competition because it took so much time, but while Ernie was still photographing, he would invite me to go out on a Sunday. When I could find the time, I would go with him.

One day he came in and said, "Wilma, would you like to go out Sunday?"

I said, "Sure."

He said, "Where shall we go?"

I said, "I just happened to be out the other evening and I saw a place I would like to go to, between here and Dufur."

Ernie asked where it was.

I explained what canyon it was in and that there was an old barn with a wagon by it and a poplar tree.

He said, "We'll go out there."

I said, "I don't know who owns it, so I don't have permission from the owner."

Ernie said, "Oh, he wouldn't care."

I asked, "Who owns it?"

He said, "I do!"

Ernie received his 640 acceptances and his coveted Five-Star Rating in Color Slides in 1967, less than ten years after joining the PSA. Wilma said, "That's a lot of pictures to send in four at a time . . . it was a record. He started from nothing. Other people work a lifetime and never reach that goal. I was absolutely amazed when he came in and said, 'Well, this should make it.' and he had a report card with his Five-Star acceptance on it."

Wilma then remembered ruefully, "He took his camera home and put it on the closet shelf and never took it down again. It just sat there."

In his later years, Ernie destroyed his beautiful pictures. Elden Wagenblast said, "I know they burnt up a bunch of them. I gave 'em heck about it. I went up there the next day and saw scraps of pictures around the fireplace. 'What are you doing that for?' I said. They said that nobody wanted them. I said the heck they did; I'd have taken them. But it is just one of those things." Ernie took pictures for his personal satisfaction, without regard for public acclamation. He had attained the goal he had set for himself, and then he allowed himself to quit. He had no immediate family to leave his slides to. In his typical, modest way, he assumed that no one else would be interested in them, so he let them go.

That was Ernie Kuck.

"A photographer today would scorn Ernie's camera as being 'old,'" said Wilma. "Jerry Jeffers, a more recent owner of Mel-O's Camera Shop, said, 'Oh, he used that awful old camera.' Does it always follow that 'new' equipment improves photography?" pondered Wilma.

In Ernie's defense, she said, "I don't know why it would; do you suppose anyone asked Hemingway what model typewriter he used?"

In a final reflection, Wilma said, "Ernie was a pretty smart man. At least he had a mind for getting ahead in the world."

Ernie and Elden Wagenblast at the Elks.
Ernie made many friends during his seventy-four years as an Elk.

*Photo courtesy of Columbia Gorge
Discovery Center*

CHAPTER 18

Ernie and Friends

Carrie enjoyed traveling. She and Ernie took a vacation to Hawaii. Perhaps the endless photographic opportunities enticed Ernie off the mainland. After the trip to Hawaii, they bought a travel trailer and joined many of their longtime friends in the Good Sam Club. The trailer allowed Carrie to "get out and go" in a setting full of Ernie's good friends. They seldom attended the local camp outs, but joined the longer trips, where Ernie positioned his rig right behind the leaders, Emery and Opal Thompson, who planned the itineraries. When on the road, Emery knew he had to gauge the green lights carefully because Ernie would run a red light rather than fall behind.

In 1982, they went on a jaunt to Death Valley; the plans included entry into Mexico for a few miles before returning to the United States further west. When Ernie learned of the plan to go into Mexico, he spoke up. He said he wasn't going to take his rig across the border—period. He would stay in his own country and meet the rest of the travelers at their point of re-entry, but *his* rig would not go to Mexico. The others didn't want to go without him. They then resolved the issue by deciding to leave all the rigs north of the border, walk into Mexico, shop, and walk back across the border. After that had been accomplished, they moved on to a successful conclusion of their trip.

Ernie liked to play cards and he was very good at it. Members of the Good Sam Club played lots of card games on trips. One player said she didn't expect to win when she played against someone who could shuffle cards like Ernie did. His friends insist that, after the first two rounds of a game, Ernie knew what everyone held in his hand. Ernie loved to win but did not always lose in a civil manner. Friends at the Elks can recall occasions when a red-faced, tight-lipped Ernie threw his cards on the table and stomped out.

Ernie Kuck loved to play pinochle and Ernie Rhodes loved to watch Ernie Kuck play. Rhodes described a game:

> He never had much to say, but he had that little grin on his face . . . I just kind of set there and would watch him when he would grin, y'know. He would set someone, and it would just tickle the tar out of him. And he'd have that little grin on his face. On the way home, I said to my wife, Mabel, "I could see Nettie Wetle all over him when we were playing pinochle together." [Nettie was Ernie's aunt.]

Ernie participated in many organizations and events in Wasco County. As a devoted member of the Elks, he attended meetings regularly and quietly underwrote many worthy projects.

He belonged to the Sheriff's Posse and practiced with the mounted drill team that performed at rodeos and parades. Once, when the sheriff was delayed talking with a Portland Rose Festival Parade official, Ernie took the initiative and organized the riders so that they were ready when the parade started.

Ernie could always be found at local rodeos wherever he was needed. He often rode as "pick-up-man" for the cowboys in the ring. Each year, the Saturday night celebration of the Fort Dalles Rodeo included a "beer bust" that lasted into the morning hours. To legally sell beer, food also had to be sold. Fortunately, as a nondrinker, Ernie was always available to man the grill.

Ernie was an admirer of fine horses, but Appaloosas were his favorites. The beautiful, spotted animals were frequently his preferred mount. One such horse, named Badger, won awards at an Appaloosa show in Idaho. Badger was not only beautiful but smart. Ernie taught him, and later another horse named Patchy, how to jump into the back of the truck—no ramp, no bank, no loading dock, they just hopped in!

In December 1938, Ernie signed the incorporation papers for the Appaloosa Horse Club, along with Claude and Faye Thompson of Moro; Dr. Francis Haines, an authority on Appaloosa horses; and Ernie's attorney, Frank Dick. The club was dedicated to preserving, promoting, and enhancing the Appaloosa breed of horses. Ernie was the first to serve as vice president of the club.

CHAPTER 19

"That's My Ernie!"

Ernie Kuck had been a faithful client of Kargl Elwood & Geiger Inc., an insurance firm in The Dalles, for give or take forty years. Ernie first worked with Doc Elwood, one of the original partners, followed by Bill Hawksley. Finally, Ernie's file was assigned to Roger Howe. Roger was one of the newer members of the company, but he was not an insurance novice. His father, Jack Howe, had been a remarkably successful insurance representative for many years, so Roger had an excellent role model.

The staff would see Ernie crossing the street toward their office and a murmur could be heard as they looked at each other. "Oh, oh! Here comes Ernie."

Said Roger:

> He was a little man and he walked with a scowl on his face. He always wore the cowboy boots and hat; sometimes I think he even wore the same kerchief. It didn't matter what he looked like or what he did. He had power. And he was probably one of the toughest guys I ever had to deal with insurance-wise. He was quite a character. I think he was intimidating to most of the public. He seemed to be aware of it, and he loved it. Everyone knew he was very well-to-do.

"That's My Ernie!"

As they became acquainted over the years, friendship developed. Roger liked Ernie and the challenge he presented. Roger made an effort to get through "that thick crust and see what was really there."

When Roger saw Ernie coming, he immediately got the Kuck file from the cabinet and had it on the counter in front of him, then greeted this longtime customer as he entered. Ernie would sound gruff—no smile, no emotion, "I need to talk about my insurance," he'd growl.

Roger would reply, "Well, let's talk."

He'd say, "Get the file."

"It's right here." And that would stump Ernie. He wouldn't give Roger the satisfaction of knowing that he recognized that Roger was ready, but Roger saw a little twinkle in his eye. In reviewing the policy, Roger's perception was that there were parts that Ernie did not really understand.

Roger observed that if Ernie didn't understand some detail, his reaction was likely, "Take it out of my policy." If Roger protested, Ernie would reply, "I don't need that house [or cabin]." The insurance company would inevitably ask why the buildings had been dropped from Ernie's policy, and they finally had to accept that those buildings were "self-insured."

Roger said, "That's my Ernie!"

In talking about the development of their friendship, Roger said:

> I would always try to get him to talk about the old days—driving the cattle through town, riding horses, and tending the saddle shop. One of the most entertaining occasions was when we went out into the country.
>
> Ernie had some property that was an older place. I had to locate some specific buildings, so he came into

town and picked me up. I was very nervous because this was when he wasn't driving very well. We were out there on the property that Bill Markman leased from Ernie [the Eight Mile ranch], and we were looking at the different buildings. Each building had a history, and Ernie knew every board and every nail. He would talk about the farmer and his father and his father's father. He was absolutely as sharp as a tack. He owned a very interesting building that had some hand-hewn beams in it, and he started talking about the old Umatilla House, just as if I knew all about it.

The feed shed made with hand-hewn beams at the Five Mile place.

Photo by Jonathan Hill courtesy of Bill Markman

By this time we were pretty good friends and he actually laughed once in a while—which was amazing, 'cause I could count on the fingers of one hand the times I had heard him laugh out loud. He went on and on talking about the old days.

"That's My Ernie!"

Finally, I said, "Ernie, I don't remember that."

He said, "I thought you were born and raised here."

I said, "Well, I was, but when were you talking about?"

He said, "Back in the '20s and '30s."

I said, "I wasn't even born until 1948!"

And he just roared. "OK, kid. Well, we'll have to do this again." I think he really enjoyed talking about the history of The Dalles. He knew all about it, and he didn't embellish it. He stuck to the facts.

CHAPTER 20

"Save Your Money"

As a little boy, Bill Markman heard his folks talk with their friends about Ernie and his activities—always positive, upbeat stories. Bill learned that Ernie was established with cattle, that he had a business in town, that he was an Elk, and that he owned lots of pasture land in the Chenowith hills. Bill reasoned that Ernie deserved the respect that he got from various members of the community.

Then, at about ten years of age, Bill went to the Wasco County Fair and Rodeo and saw Ernie for the first time, as flag bearer in the grand entry. Ernie's horse had a smooth gait and Ernie rode so well that the horse, rider, and flag appeared to be one entity. Impressed, young Bill thought that if Ernie Kuck ever found out who Bill Markman was, Bill would have found his place in the world.

An industrious kid in high school, Bill looked for a summer job on a wheat ranch. Earl Wagenblast, who leased Ernie's ranch on Eight Mile, needed help and he hired Bill. That job lasted through college and Bill really liked it. After graduating from Oregon State University, he worked for a time in Portland. However, eastern Oregon kept calling to him. He returned to The Dalles and leased a ranch from

"Save Your Money"

Clarence Quirk, but fondly remembered the Eight Mile ranch where he had worked for so many years.

When Earl Wagenblast started building a home in town for his retirement, Bill visited him. He told Earl he wanted to lease the Eight Mile ranch and told him he planned to talk to Ernie about it. Thinking that it was probably an exercise in futility, he called on Ernie and told him of his aspirations. Ernie heard him out quietly, then said, "Okay." Bill didn't know how to interpret that. The only comfort he could find in that reply was that Ernie had heard him and he did not say, "No." Bill didn't push.

One day in November 1982, Ernie drove into Bill's leased ranch. Bill thought maybe Ernie had seen a loose cow and come in to tell him. Bill invited him in. After he sat down, he abruptly asked, "So you want the place?" He pulled out his little leather book with the three metal rings and showed Bill the page that recorded when he had decided to lease the Eight Mile ranch to Bill.

Although single, Bill moved to the Eight Mile ranch and lived in the little house that the Tibbets, and later Earl Wagenblast, had occupied. Bill tended to his farming but often, when he went to town, he stopped to visit with Ernie to talk about the operation of the ranch. Bill found Ernie easy to talk to, open to new ideas, and interested in how the ranch was run. If Bill asked him about something, Ernie would just say, "If it makes you money, it makes me money."

Ernie's trademark was, "If you are going to do something, do it right—don't cut corners." Everyone knew that Ernie's word was as good as his bond.

During their many visits, Ernie sometimes related stories to Bill from his past, saying, "I've never told this to anyone before." Bill respected that confidence; he didn't want to be the one to talk out of turn. The relationship that they developed over the years revealed much about Ernie as an elder, a landlord, a mentor, and a friend.

Bill met a new nurse at the hospital. She, too, had attended OSU for one year. When Shelia Flora and Bill married in 1986, Bill talked to Ernie about buying the ranch. All Ernie said was, "Save your money."

One day during 1990, Ernie came out into the field and he and Bill kind of agreed on a price for the place based on sales of neighboring property. Ernie said that he would take care of the details. Ernie had bought and sold so many land tracts that his attorney wrote the contract in the customary form. Bill read it and had an objection to a small clause that differed from what he and Ernie had agreed on; he asked the attorney, who did not offer to change it. Bill then asked Ernie about it. The next time Bill saw the contract, it was written exactly as he and Ernie had agreed it would be.

The little house remains by the creek. Many of the original farm-type buildings are still in use; they are sound, sturdy structures. They have been modified to serve changing farm practices; the stalls for the numerous horses formerly used to harvest the crops have been converted into mangers to accommodate cattle.

Present horsepower comes in larger sizes than horses did, so doors have been enlarged to provide shelter for the farm machinery. The integrity of the building structure is noteworthy; the barns and sheds remain square and erect, years of use notwithstanding. What Ernie built was built to last! Many of the buildings carry the dates of construction followed by another date if it had been remodeled—sometimes recorded with numbers from a license plate, sometimes recorded with protruding nails outlining the digits of the year. The "Double Lazy A" brand is on some structures and some gates.

    Bill and Shelia Markman invited Ernie to their home for dinner to celebrate his ninety-third birthday. Ernie enjoyed his time with them at the Eight Mile place—the first ranch that he had purchased east of The Dalles. As Ernie prepared to leave, the Markmans asked if he would like to take the leftover pork chops home. He grinned and accepted the offer. As Ernie walked down the steps, Bill thought to himself, "There is something wrong when a multimillionaire leaves your home and all you can offer him is a couple of cold pork chops!"

One of Ernie's 1273 padlocks

*Photo by Jonathan Hill, courtesy of the
Columbia Gorge Discovery Center*

CHAPTER 21

A Lifelong Collector

Ernie, born to be a collector and a saver, had family treasures that were in storage—items such as barrels of his grandmother's china, his uncle's handmade guns, and a little stash of prescription bottles from drug stores that operated in The Dalles during the early 1900s. He couldn't remember when he didn't collect postage stamps! He also collected cowbells, padlocks, and a small display of barbed wire.

Ernie Rhodes brought his granddaughter with him one day when he visited Ernie's home. There was a big table covered with various tools, gadgets, and unrecognizable objects. The little girl went over to look at them and Ernie was right there to tell her about each piece as her grandpa sat lost in amazement. He had never heard Ernie talk that much to anyone about anything.

Ernie's interests evolved and changed as time passed. For a while, he concentrated on cowbells. He had lots of them, but finally sold them at auction when he really became interested in collecting padlocks. He mounted the padlocks on matching boards that covered the inside walls of his barn. He knew the manufacturer of each one, and he had keys for many of them. They varied in size and shape depending on what they were designed for. Lots of railroad padlocks were large and exceptionally strong. The padlocks from jails were complicated and very substantial. Ernie always appreciated help in building his collection. In the end, he had 189 boards of padlocks that he displayed in his barn.

Vernie Jarl, a construction contractor, had a passing interest in padlocks and watched for them when he visited the little second-hand stores and yard sales in areas where he worked all over Oregon. He owned some unique locks that Ernie examined several times before making an offer to buy them. Vernie sold Ernie 775 padlocks, including 55 railroad locks with keys, for $2,000. Pleased with the deal, both men continued collecting. Vernie prowled the little shops and sales and brought Ernie treasures that he had discovered. It could be truthfully said that Ernie and Vernie's friendship revolved entirely around padlocks!

Ernie's insurance agent, Roger Howe, went to the Kuck house on one occasion and saw that Ernie had a phenomenal collection of old locks. Roger took pictures of them. Ernie also owned a collection of old guns and had thousands upon thousands of dollars worth of antiques. As an insurance agent, Roger was going crazy. He told Ernie he had to get insurance on them. Ernie said, "These don't need insurance. They won't burn." Roger said he never had met anyone who had so much and who never wanted it insured. Then Roger added, "Of course, he saved a lot of money over the years."

Ernie wanted to preserve the history of Wasco County. During the 1980s, the Wasco County Court appointed a committee to explore the possibility of a museum or attraction that would encourage tourists to visit the area. In 1986, the Columbia River Gorge National Scenic Area Act was passed by

A Lifelong Collector

the U.S. Congress, eventually resulting in the allocation of $5 million for an interpretative center in a yet-to-be-determined Oregon location.

The committee began working on a proposal for the interpretative center to be located in The Dalles. They found a site west of town near Interstate 84 but needed funds to pursue options on the three separate parcels needed. It was about this time that Bill Dick, a local attorney, called Judge Bill Hulse (Wasco County CEO). Bill Dick said that there was a person in Wasco County who wanted to leave some money for a county museum. He said that this person was going to leave the majority of his estate for that purpose and he assured Judge Hulse that it would be a sizable amount of money. Shortly thereafter, $500,000 was donated for the project. Needless to say, Bill Dick was representing Ernie, who stayed in the background as a mysterious donor until his death revealed that he had created a trust to establish a Wasco County Historical Museum and had bequeathed approximately $9 million to fund it.

Ernie's attitude never changed: All the people he dealt with to accomplish his many generous deeds were sworn to secrecy—"Don't tell anyone!"

Ernie and Carrie Kuck

Photo by Patty Gray, granddaughter of Carrie Kuck.

CHAPTER 22

"Too Many Years Have Passed"

As Ernie aged, he spent less time in the saddle and didn't "ride the fence line" as often as he had in the past. One time he came upon several miles of missing fence posts—about 300 of them! Thieves had cut the wire and stolen the metal posts, leaving only those they couldn't jack out of the ground.

Occasionally, people took advantage of Ernie in his later years. When he contracted to have the timber harvested from a 6,000 acre parcel, the loggers cut the trees and cleared the land. The law required replanting after a timber harvest, but when they went in to replant they were pretty "sharp," which was to say they were dishonest. They replaced trees a few hundred yards up the hill from the road, knowing that it wasn't likely Ernie would get out of his truck and hike that hill to check up on the job.

Young people often invaded his line cabins for weekend parties, leaving the cabins in a shambles and all the emergency supplies used or destroyed. One cabin burned down. Growing up, Ernie had learned to respect other people's property; this kind of senseless vandalism baffled him.

In 1975, at Tygh Valley before the Wasco County Fair started, the director said they had asked Ernie if he would be the flag bearer for the grand entry. Ernie just shook his head and said, "Too many years have passed."

Ernie sold the last of his cattle in 1982 when he was eighty-six years old. His innovative corrals with gates and pulleys made it possible for him to gather, corral, and load out the last truckload of cattle all by himself. He still rode his horses in 1986, many of them quality Appaloosas. Eventually, he accepted the fact that he had to sell these equine friends. He arranged for the sale, and the buyer picked up all the stock except for Ernie's favorite horse. His chores lightened. Then Carrie learned that "her" horse had been sold with the lot. Oh, my! Ernie immediately tried to buy back Carrie's horse, but the man refused.

When Ernie told Elden Wagenblast what he had done, Elden said, "I'll bet it was pretty cool around there."

Ernie replied, "It was frosty."

Ernie had been a longstanding member of the Wasco County Pioneers Association, and in 1986 they honored him as Pioneer of the Year.

As time passed and age caught up with Ernie, the skillful shuffler of cards became less adept. There was one solitaire game that Frank Falbo and Ernie both enjoyed, but all the cards had to be dealt at the start of the game. Frank would deal the cards. Then, together, they would figure out the moves, usually made by Frank's more nimble fingers. If they lost the game, Frank would shuffle and deal again.

Liability insurance was important to Ernie, but it took a long time for Roger Howe to get Ernie to agree to a million-dollar policy. Roger thought Ernie didn't understand the need for so much liability insurance, but Roger knew that it was very important for somebody with Ernie's net worth to have it.

"Too Many Years Have Passed"

Finally, Ernie had to move to town. Reluctantly, he left his home on Chenowith Road and took an apartment adjacent to Carrie at a local retirement facility. Elden Wagenblast helped move him to town. As they unloaded the last items from Elden's car, Ernie left his camera on the back seat. Elden had offered to buy it from him earlier, but Ernie had never given him a definitive answer. Elden asked if he should bring the camera into Ernie's new home and Ernie said, "Naw, you take it." Elden asked what he wanted for it. "Nothin'." Elden still treasures that gift.

Bob Sallee told a story about an accident Ernie had in September of 1991 while returning from his property on Chenowith. He was driving down Doyle Grade one evening and, as Bob described it:

> It was getting towards dark, and he kinda missed the corner. He was off the road and the pickup was on its side and his passenger got out but Ernie couldn't get out. My brother came around the corner and saw headlights pointing up to the sky. There was smoke comin' up. He hopped up on top of the pickup, looked down inside, and there was Kuck down in the corner. He could not get the door open, so he just reached in there and grabbed him by the shoulders and literally just picked him up and cradled him in his arms. He took Ernie over to the road just in time to hear someone on the radio saying, "We've got a 94 year-old man here..."
>
> "Five!" Ernie corrected.

Ernie suffered several broken ribs and his passenger was injured slightly. True to form, Ernie covered all her medical expenses. It was only when Ernie came in to the insurance agency that Roger learned that this had actually been Ernie's *second* accident. Rather than jeopardize his driving privilege, Ernie said, "Forget it. I'll just write a check for it."

Friends comment that they observed a change in Ernie when he had to leave Chenowith. They did the best they could to visit with him and get him out to see changes as they happened, but he lost interest when he lost his independence.

Bill Markman visited him in his new home and, appraising the accommodations, asked, "Where is your stamp collection?" Ernie grinned, reached behind his chair, and said, "Right here." He had collected stamps his whole long life. Someone once asked him how many he had; he replied, "All of 'em." He left the stamp collection, along with his Uncle George's handmade guns, various antiques, and all of his 1,273 padlocks, to the museum that would soon be built.

Ernie's little book and a detailed map showing the parcels he had purchased from whom and for how much went to longtime friend Floyd Tibbets. He gave the bottles he had found as a child below the hospital hill to Bill and Shelia Markman, along with a pair of spurs. He gave his "Lazy Double A" branding iron to Zelta Wasson, Mannie's widow.

Ernie's final residence was in a nursing home. His attorney said he was thinking clearly until the very end. The people who knew him well felt that his death began when, for the last time, he left his beloved home on Chenowith Road.

Ernie Kuck died on March 19, 1992, at the age of ninety-five. His funeral was held at Smith Callaway Chapel and included the Elks final rites. He was buried at IOOF cemetery in the family plot. The man is gone but the memories go on.

In remembering Ernie, Paul Vogt remarked:

"Too Many Years Have Passed"

His education was limited, but he was not stupid. He was smart. . . . He was basically a loner. He kind of went his way. He didn't ask anybody's advice and he didn't tell anybody what the hell he was doing. He had his own program and he pursued it. . . . He wasn't in it to make all that money. He was interested in a way of life.

Ernie Kuck

Photo from author's personal files

APPENDIX A

E. A. KUCK LAND PURCHASES

The following list is property purchased (in the 1900's) as recorded in Ernie's "Little Book"

Date	Seller	Acres	Price
	MOSIER COUNTRY		
10/27/24	V. D. Williamson	160.00	$85.32
10/27/24	W. C. Dewey	40.00	$31.65
10/27/24	W. G. Kruger	40.00	$43.56
10/27/24	E. O. Jetty	140.40	$83.70
01/03/25	Bert W. Emerson	163.75	$750.00
06/08/25	Bert R. Wilder	99.00	$400.00
01/06/26	Lizze E. Baumann	158.87	$500.00
03/16/26	Robt. W. Simpson	240.00	$720.00
03/22/26	W. N. Evens	120.00	$360.00
07/19/26	L. H. Leninger	165.34	$45.27
07/19/26	May E. Paget	20.00	$8.89
07/19/26	Wm. T. Branch	40.00	$9.31
09/20/26	R. G. Weisbeck	40.00	$120.00
02/23/27	E. Hurst	35.00	$87.40
05/23/27	Miles C. Carter	160.00	$400.00
05/31/27	M. Barcus	40.00	$65.25
11/22/27	E. Hurst	105.00	$129.78
03/13/28	Geo. W. Kindred	120.00	$64.00
03/12/28	Edyth Gotter 5 A. bought again - 12/7/38	75.00	$14.18
03/13/28	Fowler	20.00	$14.40
03/13/28	J. C. Morley	80.00	$27.42

Date	Seller	Acres	Price
	MOSIER COUNTRY cont.		
12/27/30	W. E. Chown	86.50	$98.95
07/02/28	J. L. Davidson	160.00	$480.00
07/18/28	Mt. Dell Orchard Tracts	56.67	$50.88
11/01/28	G. D. Montague	160.00	$480.00
09/26/28	L. G. Clarke	40.00	$108.00
04/17/30	R. J. Lewis	80.00	$282.25
05/07/29	Nettie Ricketts	40.00	$120.00
10/24/29	W. R. Stokes, Jr.	320.00	$800.00
04/23/30	E. C. Denton	20.00	$52.50
03/26/31	Harry H. Stout	160.00	$36.94
03/26/31	Willamette Trust & Inv. Co.	140.00	$75.93
03/26/31	Clyde E. Smith	5.00	$11.22
03/26/31	Mt. Dell Orchard Tracts	9.70	$6.91
11/21/33	Frank E. Crum	160.00	$27.28
11/21/33	E. W. Paget	40.00	$12.86
11/21/33	L. Paget	20.00	$6.46
11/21/33	L. T. Wilcox	160.60	$25.67
11/21/33	C. E. Glander	40.00	$7.13
11/21/33	E. Hildreth (sold 6 A $25.00)	160.00	$23.49
12/01/36	O.W.J.S.L. BK.	2680.25	$5000.00 +$876.32 (back taxes)
06/05/37	Fredrickson	196.98	$110.00 +$185.50 (back taxes)

Appendix A

Date	Seller	Acres	Price
	MOSIER COUNTRY cont.		
06/10/37	C. L. Gavin	160.00	$280.00
01/22/38	E. C. Phirman sold 372.28A $353.67	712.28	$675.97
07/22/38	Marietta Hildreth Abernathey	160.60	$200.00
07/23/38	Clyde Austin	40.00	$20.00
12/07/38	Alice A. Dwight	20.00	$6.45
12/07/38	Laura E. Frenok	160.00	$33.06
12/07/38	Edyth Gotter (E.A.K. Bought 3/12/28 from County in Edyth Gotter Deed but foreclosed again due to error)	5.00	$7.06
12/07/38	Thomas Rash	20.00	$30.43
12/07/38	Becker and Combs	160.00	$134.44
12/07/38	C. E. Moulton	120.00	$49.30
12/07/38	H. T. Sprague	45.78	$27.18
12/07/38	A. H. Spraner (Deeded 80 A. to J. Huskey - 1955)	156.31	$142.60
12/07/38	E. L. Thompson	160.00	$29.85
12/10/38	Emma S. Christman	178.00	$795.00
03/27/39	E. H. Pratt	160.00	$200.00
11/20/39	Frank Kindred	120.00	$150.00
03/06/40	Frank D. Layton	160.00	$500.00
04/02/40	C. E. Copple	118.42	$296.05
05/22/40	Elsie Bender	1.50	$20.00
08/22/40	S. D. Wilkerson	80.00	$48.93

Date	Seller	Acres	Price
	MOSIER COUNTRY cont.		
08/02/41	Frank, Roy, and Tom Pratt	161.00	$202.50
		40.00	$75.35
09/29/41	State of Oregon	103.06	$210.00
01/10/42	James T. Wood	160.00	$116.75
01/22/42	Eugenia H. Taggert	160.00	$20.00
		40.00	+$134.22 (back taxes)
Feb 51	Exchanged 243.8 A to Wm. D. Ketchum for 243.38A from Wm. D. Ketchum		
09/21/42	Walter E. Bliss	160.00	$200.00
03/18/44	Wasco County	25.70	$32.13
07/15/44	Stebco Inc.	900.00	$1,233.00
03/27/45	William Sendlinger	160.00	$240.00
05/24/45	Stevenson	603.79	$754.74
07/27/45	Geo. Chamberlain	378.49	$473.11
08/23/47	R. J. Stearns	319.09	$398.86
09/29/47	Geo. Chamberlain	80.00	$100.00
09/29/47	Beauford Clemmons	73.31	$91.64
03/30/48	Delaney P. Schanno (11/01/64 Sold to Ed Hines)	107.15	$160.00
05/05/49	Wasco County/J.F. Huebner	160.00	$253.95
05/05/49	Wasco County/C.M Dickenson	160.00	$650.00
11/14/49	G. W. and P.S. Sellers (O'Connor Place)	200.00	$1,600.00
12/13/49	H. E. Willerton	30.77	$67.50
10/04/50	Geo. C. Durham	160.00	$1,000.00
10/04/50	Mead and Wade	50.00	$450.00

Appendix A

Date	Seller	Acres	Price
	MOSIER COUNTRY cont.		
02/28/51	Matilda B. Kennedy	160.00	$1,300.00
07/09/51	Tom Kennen	40.00	$200.00
07/09/51	Tum-a-Lum Lumber Co.	80	$200.00
09/14/54	J. S. Courtney	140.55	$140.55
12/14/54	Christopher Co. (Land, $480; Timber, $3,520)	160.00	$4,000.00
1955	Deeded to John Huskey	80.00	
08/01/56	Stebco. Inc	280.00	$280.00
01/14/59	Avery B. Ashley	110.00	$1,100.00
11/01/64	Ed. Hines Lumber Co.	829.40	$2,743.20
05/09/68	Forest Brokers Inc.	60.00	$7,500.00
	MILL CREEK LAND		
08/22/45	Willow Spring - Hill	280.00	$700.00
08/22/45	Schoolmom [sic] Spring - Hill	160.00	$400.00
02/14/47	Wasco County	81.26	$50.00
11/12/47	Merel F. Jewell	169.04	$211.30
11/24/47	John Gavin	484.97	$606.25
04/09/48	C. A. Pembroke	127.10	$158.88
04/26/48	John H. Sellers	320.00	$480.00
05/05/49	Grand Aerie Eagles	160.00	$300.00
05/05/49	Wasco Co. Lampert Imp. Co.	165.95	$350.00
05/05/49	Wasco Co. Bertha Day	160.00	$158.80
09/06/50	Wasco Co. Beard	80.00	$241.84

Remembering Ernie Kuck

Date	Seller	Acres	Price
	MILL CREEK LAND cont.		
09/01/50	Claire Mears	162.09	$1,150.00
10/02/50	Bertha E. Glenn (Sold – Ed Hines 11/01/64)	160.00	$400.00
10/06/50	J. L. Workman	280.00	$1,200.00
10/23/50	Catherine Turner	160.00	$1,000.00
11/28/50	J. A. Robbins	160.00	$800.00
06/09/51	Dale F. Hammond	120.00	$250.00
08/09/51	Lillie and J.W. Tindall	280.00	$2,000.00
01/16/53	Dalles City	1008.90	$10,089.00
02/06/53	Ed Sandoz	160.00	$1,600.00
02/16/54	Julius A. Ulrich	164.08	$4,000.00
	Hansell O. Wilds	183.60	$1,836.00
05/10/56	Stebco Inc.	160.00	$1,600.00
06 -- 57	Mrs. I. B. McKenzie	20.00	$200.00
	HOOD RIVER COUNTY		
05/01/48 11/01/64	Emily Hall Coiner Cedar Swamp (Sold 120A to Ed Hines Lumber Co.)	160.00	$200.00
06/23/51 11/01/64	W.E. McNeill Owens Place (Sold to Ed Hines Lumber Co.)	480.00	$3,300.00
11/01/64	Ed Hines Lumber Co.	0.50	$5.00
	GILPIN RANCH		
03/02/25	Lois Gilpin	1932.70	$30,000.00
09/19/49	Delaney McKensie	10.00	$50.00
02/08/50	Grant Cyphers	391.04	$12,500.00
10/01/51	John S. Robinson	11.80	$2,000.00

Appendix A

Date	Seller	Acres	Price
	DESCHUTES RANCH		
	Harry and Ernie inherited from H. L. and Minnie Kuck	1693.84 1240.00	$43,000.00 tillable acres
	MISCELLANEOUS LAND		
05/06/55	Webbers (house on Chenowith)	162.64	$37,000.00
02/28/57	Fred Wetle	160	$1,600.00
01/01/74	Anderson Ranch/Fred Wetle [inherited] Creek Land Hill Land assessed value	156.11 160.77 316.88	$24,636.00

APPENDIX B

Water Sources

This list is from Ernie's "Little Book." Each water source also had notes that included such things as the date, who worked on it, costs, survey coordinates, and dated notes if the source went dry, or had water all year, if it was rebuilt and when, by whom, and costs.

1.	1941	South Pasture Pond
2.	1941	North Pasture Pond
3.	1947	Phirman Pond
4.	1941	Smith Pond
5.	1948	Buckhorn Pond
		1953 Dams (5)
6.	1953	Sawdust
7.	1953	Buck Hollow
8.	1953	Layton
9.	1953	Mud Spring
10.	1953	Rock Elery
11.	1954	Stebco Pond
12.	1959	Sam Johns Pond
13.	1959	Baker Canyon Pond
14.	1959	Kruger Pond
15.	1961	Oregon Pond
16.	1963	Buck Canyon Pond
17.	1963	Simpson Pond
18.	1963	Movey Ridge Pond & Trail
19.	1963	Mutton Camp Pond
20.	1964	Marin Basin Pond
21.	1964	Redel Pond

22.	1964	Lucky Canyon Pond
23.	1964	Bear Camp Pond
24.	1964	Forest Boundary Pond
25.	1965	Crum Ridge Pond
26.	1966	Goat Trail Pond
27.	1966	Britten Pond
28.	1966	Eagle Pond
29.	1966	Rhodes Cistern
30.	1967	Elk Pond
31.	1967	Hans Olsen Pit
32.	1967	Sheldon Well Pit
33.	1968	Jasper Pond
34.	1968	Browns Creek Pond
35.	1969	Big Pine Basin Pond
36.	1968	Wire Corral Pond
37.	1969	Denton Pond
38.	1970	Kennedy Pond
39.	1970	Milk Can Pond
40.	1972	Lightening Ridge Pond
41.	1972	Lady Slipper Pond
42.	1972	Wilcox Pond

Small Spring Fed Ponds

1.	1956	Freeman Spring
2.	1956	Coon Spring
3.	1958	Cooper Spring
4.	1959	Saddle Back Spring
5.	1960	Willow Spring
6.	1963	Schoolmarm Spring
7.	1963	Burnt Crossing Spring
8.		Bee Spring

Appendix B

9. 1964 Godberson Well
10. 1966 B.L.M. Buck Canyon
11. 1976 Rabbit (Don's)
12.   Little Jasper

Pasture Springs

1. 1929 Leininger, cement
2. 1936 Dunigan, cement
3. 1958 Coon, pond
4. 1969 Freeman, pond
5. 1969 Martin, steel tank
6. 1970 Poe
7. 1938 Schlueter, cement
8. 1969 O'Connor, steel tank
9. 1938 Twin, cement
10. 1939 Cotton, cement
11.   Basin
12. 1938 Oak, log trough
13. 1938 Sheep, cement
14. 1975 Bill Spencer
15. 1952 Wade
16.   Meed
17. 1976 Rabbit (Don's), pond
18. 1968 Little Jasper, pond

Author's note: There appears to be some overlap between the two lists of springs. They are listed here as Ernie recorded them in his "Little Book."

CPSIA information can be obtained at www.ICGtesting.com
Printed in the USA
BVOW07s1049130515

399720BV00001B/1/P